Marketing the Primary School
An Introduction for Teachers and Governors

Resources in Education

Other titles in this Series:

Resources in Education

Marketing the Primary School

An Introduction for Teachers and Governors

Brian Hardie MA DLC

Northcote House

British Library Cataloguing in Publication Data
Hardie, Brian
   Marketing the primary school : an introduction for teachers
   and governors. - (Resources in education).
   1. England. Primary schools. Marketing
   I. Title II Series
   372.942

   ISBN 0-7463-0591-5

First published in 1991 by Northcote House Publishers Ltd,
Plymbridge House, Estover Road, Plymouth PL6 7PZ, United
Kingdom. Tel: Plymouth (0752) 705251. Fax: (0752) 777603.
Telex: 45635.

Typeset by PDQ Typesetting, Stoke-on-Trent
Printed in Great Britain by BPCC Wheatons Ltd, Exeter

Contents

Preface

The Local Management of Schools and the Education Reform Act are already having far-reaching implications for primary schools. With resourcing linked to the size of the pupil roll, primary school managers will need to think very carefully about the relationship between their school and the local community.

This book has been written to give a simple and clear explanation of what is necessary to do in practical terms to market the Primary School. Rather than provide a technical manual or academic work this book is firmly designed for the non-specialist. It is aimed at those who have done little or no marketing at all. It is also aimed at those who have begun consciously to manage the reputation of the school and who would now like to go further. It is expected that the reader may be a person who is interested in improving the promotion of the school and who might need the answer to a specific problem. Although it is recommended that the whole marketing process is followed, the chapters have been written to focus on specific issues.

To assist the reader at all stages each chapter includes suggested practical activities. There are more of these than any one person or group is likely to want or need. The reason is simply to provide as much choice as possible and the reader can select those which are most appropriate for his or her school at any one particular time. The book is therefore designed to be used as a handbook and returned to as different activities are needed.

The reader may be a teacher, governor or a Head who is concerned with the task of managing the reputation of the school. It is hoped that this handbook will have something for all of these different people, and their differing needs.

Acknowledgements

I should like to thank many of the staff at the Centre for Eduction Management at Crewe + Alsager College of Higher Education, especially Chris Braund for his ideas on distinctiveness and Corrie Giles for the ideas on quality.

My thanks also to the head teachers who devised the activity on evaluation who were on a 20 Day Management Course arranged by Crewe + Alsager College for Stockport LEA and to CLASP for giving permission to reproduce their brochure.

Finally, I should like to thank Roland Seymour for his editorial assistance through the various drafts of this book.

1
The Context

Marketing of our schools and of education, and in particular state education, *does* concern us all, whether we like it or not. Many teachers, and headteachers especially, may say, 'But I came into education to teach children; I didn't come into education to spend all my time selling the school!'

Things have changed quite radically since many of us started to teach and those changes have been greatest in the last few years. The point is made by Mike Moran, a headteacher, as quoted in *The Independent* of 14.12.89:

> Our roots still need to be in the classroom; our credibility as heads is definitely related to our knowledge of what goes on there. I would resist any notion that these days we are doing a different job, needing different qualities. The abilities a head needs are exactly the same as they've always been. The only thing that has changed is the way they are channelled.

The way that we channel what we are doing may make all the difference between a good school and a really successful school. Survival is vital for all concerned with your school and it is up to you to ensure this survival. Hopefully this book will give some of the answers and ideas as to how you might go about the task of making yours a successful school which will survive into the next century at least.

This chapter will be divided into a number of sections, as will all the chapters in this book, to help focus on particular issues. The issues considered here follow the journalist's six questions, Why? What? Who? When? How? and Where? with an additional section on the place of marketing. They are:

- *Why* market?
- The place of marketing within the school
- *What* is marketing?
- *Who* is the school marketing to?

- *When* should we market the school?
- *How* can we market the school?
- *Where* should we market the school?

WHY MARKET?

Survival

As mentioned earlier the first answer to 'why market?' is the one of survival in the rapidly changing environment in which we find ourselves today. Building public support for schools is not something an effective Headteacher does 'on the side'. It should, in fact, be the first act of survival. Today's reality is that schools must queue up with other public services and plead for their share of taxes. Taxpayers have become more sceptical of the educational establishment; whether directly or through those elected by them, they demand clear answers to such questions as

- What are you going to do with the money? and
- What did you do with the money we gave you last year?

The answers to these questions, and the way they are communicated, could spell the difference in individual cases between adequate and inadequate school funding. The art of building public support, therefore, has become the art of survival.

Today's Headteacher no longer has the luxury of withdrawing from the political arena with the classic apology 'My job is education'. Headship today involves politics and requires effective communications, both internally and externally, and most successful Heads have learned to master the necessary political skills.

Competency in 'building support for schools', essential for successful Headteachers, involves primarily the mastery of the art of communication and includes the following skills:

- developing and implementing school/community and school/ staff public relations;
- understanding and using the politics of governing and operating schools;
- communicating and projecting an articulate position for education;
- understanding the role and function of mass media in shaping and forming opinions;
- understanding conflict mediation and developing the skills to

accept and cope with inherent controversies.

'Public relations' is not listed first by chance. It is, in its broader sense, the one function that encompasses all the others. Those skilled in 'politics' must also be skilled in 'public relations'.

The protective LEA
Ever since declining pupil rolls hit schools ten or more years ago they have been in competition for pupils to a greater or lesser extent. In the 1980s this competition was restricted as LEAs protected schools by

- not closing schools when they could. This has meant that costs per pupil have risen;
- maintaining artificial school numbers. Restrictions by the LEA on going over or under certain numbers.

This will change radically in the near future as a result of the 1988 Education Act.

The Education Acts of the 1980s
There have been trends in the Education Acts of the 1980s which have been leading towards this change.

1980 Education Act
Parents were given the **right to choose** the school they wanted for their child, although the LEA could refuse on the grounds of inefficient use of resources and parents could appeal.

Parents were given **rights to be represented** on school governing bodies. LEAs and school governors were required to provide information to parents on such matters as criteria for admission, exam results, curriculum, discipline and organisation.

The **assisted places scheme** helped parents to increase their choice by sending their children to independent schools.

It restricted the rights of LEAs to refuse to provide primary, secondary or further education for pupils or students not belonging to their area.

1981 Education Act
This was mainly about **Special education,** but gave parents the right to be consulted about the whole of the process involving any child with Special educational needs and to appeal against an LEA's decision about appropriate provision.

1986 Education Act
This Act required every maintained school to have a **governing body** and to set up a formula for the numbers of parent, voluntary body and LEA representatives on that governing body. Parent representation was strengthened. The Act required governors to present an annual report to the parents at the school and to arrange a meeting with them to discuss it.

1988 Education Act
Here one of the stated aims of the National Curriculum is to allow for mobility of parents; with **open enrolment** parents may send their children to any school that has room for them.

With **Local Management of Schools** (LMS) funding arrangements, more pupils will bring in benefits but not additional costs. In total the capacity of a school to attract and retain pupils will be the main measure of its success.

The implications

'Choice' for parents
The 'choice' for parents has been gradually increased throughout the 1980s. This has culminated in the 1988 Act with the concept of open enrolment. This allows parents to 'shop around' and will almost certainly put pressure on *all* schools to promote themselves effectively.

Parents' views of schools have been summarised as follows:

- Schools that treat parents as partners and value their support in achieving the goals set for their children will have a good chance of surviving.

- Schools that encourage parents to value education, motivate their children to want to learn and preach the 'gospel of success' will themselves succeed.

- Schools should identify areas that concern most parents.

- Schools will have to justify their organisation and demonstrate that they really do stretch their pupils to their maximum levels of attainment.

Parents will become increasingly intolerant of the indiscipline of a few children who cause problems for the others.

- Parents will have much more power whether as parents choosing schools or as governors taking ultimate responsibility for the direction of schools.

- Schools will have to come to terms with the implications of 'parent power' and understand that it might force them to rethink patterns of organisation in a way considered impossible only a short while ago.

LMS and the declining protection of the LEA
Under LMS, schools, through their governors, will have a greater responsibility for their own finances. This could well mean that LEAs will be encouraged, or even obliged, to close undersubscribed schools. Individual schools will need to seek pupils to maintain or increase the service they are able to offer.

Unfair competition
Competition between schools, however, will not be on even ground for the following reasons:

1. **The location of schools** is not something which can be changed. The areas in which they are placed will benefit schools in the more prosperous areas and work against those in 'less desirable' areas. The support of local industry and commerce, or the lack of it, will have a profound effect on the pattern of sponsorship and links with industry. LEAs will not be able to close all 'unpopular' schools as some schools will have to be kept open for geographical or social reasons. Schools can only be closed by the Secretary of State, but the DES can be slow and is often influenced by parental lobbying.

2. **Some parents will not be able to benefit from parental choice.** Each school has a physical limit on its capacity to admit more pupils and some parents may therefore simply be 'unlucky'. Some parents are not interested in shopping around and others cannot afford the transport costs.

3. **Many parents WILL exercise their choice** and this book is about those parents and how the school can positively react to the

challenge that this creates. A fact of life in the marketplace where schools will find themselves is that schools *must* market to hold their position, or die. Nevertheless schools that concentrate on marketing to the exclusion of all else will also fail. Schools must concentrate firstly on the education which is provided for pupils, and then think about telling others how well they are doing that task.

THE PLACE OF MARKETING IN THE SCHOOL

School Development Plans (SDPs)
Schools are producing School Development Plans (SDPs) as a result of the 1988 Education Act. It is suggested that these should be *working documents* to which all those in the school constantly refer. The individual plans, which are a part of the School Development Plan, might include

- a Curriculum Development Plan
- a Staff Development Plan
- an In-Service (INSET) Development Plan and
- almost certainly a Financial Development Plan as a part of the LMS arrangements.

It is suggested that

- a Marketing Plan

should also be a part of this process. The details of how to go about producing a Marketing Plan will be discussed later.

All these constituent plans might fit together into the School Development Plan as illustrated opposite.

The three areas which are essential to help organisations give themselves 'the marketing edge' are Culture, Creativity and Commitment. Much of the work in this field has been done with successful companies in industry, but there are many ideas which can be transferred to schools.

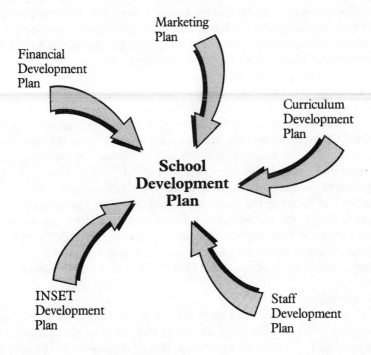

Figure 1.1 The School Development Plan

Culture

In essence, the successful marketing culture is one which is fully oriented to *identifying* what needs to be done to be successful in the market and in *doing* what is necessary to achieve it. In other words, 'Doing the right things right'.

Culture in a school means promoting a responsive culture that is market rather than product oriented, user oriented rather than seller oriented and customer driven rather than operations driven. All of these mean looking outwards into the environment towards the parents' and the children's needs rather than being concerned with making life simpler for those inside the school such as the teachers or the office staff.

Trying to change the culture within a school is not easy, but as things are changing very fast it is up to those who are managing the schools to change the attitudes of the teaching and non-teaching staff towards this 'new' way of looking at the school.

Creativity

Creativity pervades the whole thinking of the successful company, which constantly strives for better and more imaginative ways of doing things. Above all, it looks for creative insights into the environment in which it operates and the influences affecting it – economic, social, political, technological and competitive. It produces products and services to match this changing environment which are better or more suitable than those offered by competitors. Increasingly, the success of the school will depend on the level of creativity and how much it is an integral part of the school's culture. School staff must be encouraged to be creative and, when they do come up with new ideas, these must be discussed and developed.

Commitment

A common factor in successful schools is a strong commitment to success and an ability to make things happen. The commitment of school staff may have to be increased. One of the ways to do this is by a strongly positive attitude towards INSET. The new funding arrangements by the Local Education Authority Training Grants Scheme (LEATGS), previously Grant Related In-service Training (GRIST), and the introduction of 'Training Days' have increased the *amount* of in-service training, but have they increased the *quality*? Motivating people is critical to the success and growth of the school and commitment starts at the top and permeates the whole organisation.

WHAT IS MARKETING?

Kotler and Fox in *Strategic Marketing for Educational Institutions* have called marketing: 'The skills of planning and managing the institution's exchange relations with its various publics.'

The idea included within this definition is that the activity should be *planned*. This has already been indicated as a part of the School Development Plan and will be emphasised throughout this book. This is also true for the concept of *managing the process*. If marketing is *not* planned and managed then it will be at best reactive and at worst non-existent. Exchange relations emphasise the *two way communications* which are seen as essential. The final point about *various publics* emphasises both the variety of people who are involved and the fact that there is not one market, but a whole series of markets.

Public relations or marketing *is* practised to some degree in every school in the country, although it may be called something else— school community relations, public information, or communications with parents. Several decades ago school public relations were defined as a 'co-operative development and maintenance of efficient two-way channels of information and understanding between the school, its personnel and the community'. This brings out the *co-operative* nature of the exercise, in addition to the areas mentioned previously. Now it is seen as a 'dynamic process' combining these ideas and practices:

- A way of life expressed daily by the staff members in their personal relations with colleagues, pupils, parents, and the people in the community.

- A planned and continuing series of activities for communicating with both internal and external publics concerning the purposes, needs, curriculum and accomplishments of a school.

- A planned and continuing series of activities for determining what citizens think of the school and the aspirations they hold for the education of their children.

- The active involvement of citizens in the decision-making process of a school so that essential improvements may be made to their educational programme and adjustments brought about to meet the climate of social change.

The key words in this definition are **planned** and **continuing**, meaning that public relations does not just happen. It is the result of conscious effort by the school starting with the development and adoption of a policy by the governors and the staff of the school. Having started the process it is one which has to be implemented and then continued over a period of years.

If communication is not planned, it becomes haphazard or simply does not get done. Getting feedback from both staff and community through surveys, advisory groups, key communicators and other means keeps a school close to those it serves. Effective internal communication is a must, since public relations is effective only when it works from the inside out. Every employee must understand his or her important communication responsibilities. Also, if staff members don't know what the goals are and what their responsibilities are in meeting those goals, the school will never reach them.

The understanding of the environment and an audit of what we are doing now together with strategy and the development of a marketing plan are also important parts of the communications process. If issues are not identified early and appropriate strategies developed, then *they* end up managing the school system instead of vice versa.

Models of marketing
Marketing is *not* about selling a product; it is about **selling the benefits** that come with the product. It goes without saying that if you lie about the benefits then the buyers can rapidly desert the product.

There are a number of models of the stages which the buyer goes through in making the decision to buy a product. Once again, although these have been taken from the industrial and commercial world, they can help the way we think about the process that parents might go through in choosing a school. Three different models can be presented, to give comparisons and to provide some ideas and thoughts for marketing in the school.

The first of these models is self explanatory:

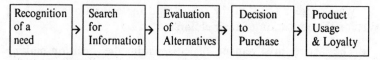

Three different models have been combined in one table to indicate the commonality at different stages.

Name of process	Decision process	AIDA	Product adoption
Various Stages of the processes	Need recognition	Attention	Awareness
	Search	Interest	Interest
	Evaluation of alternatives	Desire	Evaluation
	Desire to purchase	Action	Trial
	Usage		Adoption

Table 1.1   Models of the choice process

Basic questions which arise from these models are:

- Why do some parents choose this school?
- Why do some parents NOT choose this school?

An American commercial study confirmed that nearly 70% of customers who switched suppliers did so because of 'lousy service'. Only a small minority gave cost or existence of a better product as a reason. Is this idea transferable to education?

A final idea on 'what is marketing?' is the concept that the whole process is about **quality**. The stages of a marketing focus are therefore:

- The provision of quality
- Quality monitoring
- Quality control
- Quality improvement
- The display of quality

This is a model which is particularly appropriate to education and the marketing of schools, because it starts with the *provision* of a quality education. This is followed by the monitoring and control of that quality which in turn is seen as a developmental process in order to *improve* that quality even further. Following these four stages and only at this stage are we proud to display and talk about that quality to others.

WHO IS THE SCHOOL MARKETING TO?

A preliminary list of those to whom the school is marketing might include: pupils, parents, LEAs and even ultimately employers, FE and HE institutions and national government. A better definition might be to 'those who use the institution directly in order to gain the satisfaction of complex wants and needs'. We need to understand in more detail, though, who needs to be involved if schools are to be successful. An identification of the **internal** and **external publics** is useful.

Internal publics
The internal publics might include:

- **teachers**
  full-time
  part-time
  supply
  peripatetic

- **non-teaching staff**

secretary or clerical assistants
caretaker
cleaning staff
cooks and those who prepare meals
lunch-time supervisors

- **children**

- **governors**

There seems to be no problem when we start to identify the internal public of the school, but as soon as we consider it in detail we find that it is not as easy as we might have at first imagined. Should part time teachers be included? Probably yes, but do you include supply teachers and peripatetic staff? All of them? Even those who come in for one day only? If we are going to do this job properly, perhaps we ought to do so, but it is important for *you* to decide for yourself what is appropriate in your school. Make a list of the names.

A similar problem arises when we look at the non-teaching staff. Do you include all the part-time cleaners for example?

Perhaps there is no problem with the children, but do you include the governors as internal to the school? Under the new regulations they have the power to 'hire and fire', so they could be seen as employers and so external to the school. Once more you will have to decide for yourself what is appropriate for your school.

External publics
Involving and working with many sectors of the community is essential. These sectors or external publics include:

- parents
- Governors

- non-parents
- taxpayers
- members of the business community
- older citizens
- volunteers
- pressure groups
- community leaders
- the residential community

- County Council members

- District Council members

- LEA officers
- Local inspectorate
- HMI
- DES

- Feeder schools, such as playgroups, nursery schools, infant schools
- Schools that follow, such as secondary schools or junior schools
- Employers

- the news media
- a host of others

This list is almost endless and there is likely to be overlap between these groups, but there are also differences, some subtle, some major, between their perceptions.

Top of the list are the parents, as these are probably the largest group in the external public, but it may be that you consider that the parents should be included in the internal public and similarly with the governors.

To a certain extent it does not matter which list they are on, except that there may be seen to be a difference when we start to consider how we market the school later in the book.

The, perhaps unusual, inclusion on the list is that of the *non-parent*. Many of the people involved with the school are *not* parents of children in the school, may *not* be parents of children of school age or may *not* have children at all. They are still likely to be influential members of the community and ones with which the school may need to communicate.

PARENT/CHILD MIX
Some teachers might argue that the parent is the most important person that the school is marketing to. Many primary teachers might argue that the main person to whom they are responsible is the child. Throughout this book the *parent and child will be considered as one unit*. The reason is that the parent's view of the school is affected by the views of the child and what he or she says happens in school. Similarly the child's view of education is likely to reflect that of the parent. The two are so intertwined that they are impossible to separate, hence the idea of the parent/child as one.

Having said that, within the unit there is likely to be a varying influence according to the age of the child. When the child is young the influence of the parent is likely to be greater. When the child, student or young person is making decisions about say university the parent's influence will probably have declined. In between there is a mixture of the two to a greater or lesser extent. This might be expressed in the following diagram:

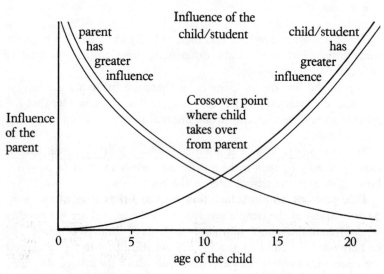

Figure 1.2. The parent/child mix

WHEN SHOULD WE MARKET THE SCHOOL?

It is useful to look at what is happening in marketing schools at the moment. Hughes, Wikeley and Nash conducted a telephone survey of 100 primary Heads in a large LEA. The main results were as follows:

- Three quarters of the Heads saw parents as consumers, although many added that they were not altogether in sympathy with this perspective. Others saw the children as consumers rather than their parents. This may confirm the view of the parent/child mix expressed earlier.

- Only one in five Heads claimed to have introduced a new policy, such as uniform, specifically because the parents wanted it – most said that parents exerted little or no pressure of that kind on the school. Indeed there were more complaints of apathy than of undue pressure.

- About one quarter of the Heads said they were actively marketing their school, mentioning glossy brochures, notices in estate agents, features in the local press and TV, and the occasional video. At least two schools had a governor with specific responsibility for public relations.

- About one third saw themselves as passively marketing, that is simply trying to spread the good name of the school through one means or another.

- **Nearly half did not believe they marketed the school at all**.

This may be because they were essentially in a seller's market. Although most reported that their parents had a fair degree of choice, few were concerned about them taking their children elsewhere: 'We're full' and 'We're oversubscribed already' were common responses. The idea that parents will go elsewhere if standards do not improve – a central assumption of the market approach to education – was clearly not regarded as a major threat by the majority in the survey.

Parents were for the most part seen as knowing little about the National Curriculum. Fewer than one in eight of the Heads thought their parents were 'well informed'; many blamed the media for 'misinforming' parents about the reality of its implementation – 'They read the papers and think it's all up and running'. Only a minority thought their parents actually wanted to know more.

Despite this apparent apathy, almost all the Heads thought that parents needed to be given more information about the National Curriculum 'if only to put right what they've learnt from the *Daily*

Mail.' Most schools had already taken active steps to do this – leaflets had been sent home, meetings had been held or were being planned, and displays had been mounted in the school. Despite – or maybe because of – their limited knowledge of the National Curriculum, most Heads believed parents were predominantly in favour of it.

Almost all the Heads thought that parents had a role to play in implementing the curriculum. For the most part this was limited to providing general support and encouragement, although some suggested that parents could be directly involved in helping their children with specific attainment targets.

Nearly two thirds of the Heads said that parents could definitely make a contribution to assessment; only one in eight gave an unequivocal 'no' to this idea. The contribution was mostly in terms of the parents providing background information about their children's ability and behaviour outside school, particularly if the school carried out baseline assessments when the children started at five.

Heads were asked to predict whether the National Curriculum and assessment would change the relationship between parents and schools. Fewer than one in ten gave a clear 'no' to this question; most thought that the changes were possible or likely.

It would seem from this evidence that some Heads are already taking part in some marketing of the school, but that if you want to 'get ahead in the game', *now* may be the time to start!

HOW CAN WE MARKET THE SCHOOL?

Later chapters deal with this in detail, but it is worth stating here that it is probably better to manage the introduction of the marketing approach into the school using the 'Slow creep' rather than the 'Big bang'. In other words introduce the marketing process gently and slowly, trying out one or two of the ideas in this book; when these have been successful, introduce some more, rather than trying to do it 'all in one go'.

As suggested earlier, incorporate a Marketing Plan into the School Development Plan and make it a part of the annual management 'cycle'.

Finally remember that it is not a 'one off', but an ongoing *process.*

WHERE SHOULD WE MARKET THE SCHOOL?

The final question in this chapter is perhaps easily answered by saying *everywhere*! The internal and external markets of the school were considered earlier in this chapter and these, in general, are the places to market the school. Once activities are seen and understood as 'marketing opportunities' then the sky is the limit. However, one must always be aware of the possibility of 'overkill' and that it is possible to 'turn people off' by being too aggressive in the marketing of the school.

Activities

Some of the questions which have been asked in this chapter are now presented in a form which may make them easier to use as activities.

CULTURE, CREATIVITY AND COMMITMENT

Culture

What changes in the school have been made in the past term (or year)?

Which of these were in response to 'outside' influences?

Change   *Influence which prompted the change*

Creativity

In what ways are staff encouraged to be creative?

Creative objective   *How encouraged*

What changes have been made in the last term (or year) *as a direct result* of ideas from the staff?

Change   *Staff who contributed ideas*

Commitment

What is being done at the moment to increase staff commitment?

Method   *Results*

What training have you had in the last term? Who has led this training?

Activity   *Leader*

THE CHOICE PROCESS

Using this model of the choice process, what *could you be doing* to 'help' your parents choose your school?

- Need recognition
- Search for information
- Evaluation of alternatives
- Decision to purchase
- Product usage and loyalty

Need recognition
What educational 'needs' do the parents have?
Type of need   *How identified*

Search for information
What information could you provide?
Information   *Source of information*

Evaluation of alternatives
What other schools could the parents choose?
What are their strengths and weaknesses?
Schools   *Strengths*   *Weaknesses*

Decision to purchase
What are the reasons why someone should choose your school?
Reason

Product usage and product loyalty
What could you do to encourage loyalty to your school?
Action   *Why effective*

QUALITY

These activities are all about the *quality* of the education provided in the school.

The provision of a quality education
What are the ways in which you provide a *quality* education?
What provided   *How provided*

Quality monitoring
In what ways do you monitor, check, evaluate the *quality* of this education?
Aspect monitored   *How monitored*

Quality control
In what ways do you control, manage, ensure the *quality* of the education?
Aspect provided   *How controlled for quality*

Quality improvement
In what ways are you trying to improve the *quality* of the education AT THE MOMENT?
Aspect   *How improved*

Displaying that quality
In what ways are you displaying *quality*?
Aspect   *How displayed*

WHO IS THE SCHOOL MARKETING TO?

Internal publics
Who are the *internal* publics of the school?
  Category   *Approx. numbers*

External publics
Who are the *external* publics of the school?
  Category   *Approx. numbers*

Having written these lists:

- Go back and underline those that *you* think are particularly important.

- Identify for each of those publics the communications channels and involvement activities that will lead to understanding and support.

- Select one internal and one external public of great importance to the school; list what individual members of that public need to understand if the school is to be successful.

2
Reputation Management

In this chapter on managing the reputation of the school there will be overlap with other chapters in terms of the *content*. There is, however, a major difference in terms of *attitude*. The sections of this chapter will be:

- The difference between reputation management and marketing
- Research into reputation
- Working together
- Representing reality

THE DIFFERENCE BETWEEN REPUTATION MANAGEMENT AND MARKETING

The first difference between reputation management and marketing has already been stated: it is that of **attitude**. Reputation management is seen as a co-operative activity. It is one where we are looking for ways to work together and share in common actions for the common good. It is essentially a passive, softer way of going about what we do. Marketing, on the other hand, might be seen as an essentially hard activity where we are in competition with others; it is very much more active, some might argue even aggressive.

Rather than seeing these as *opposites*, I should like to suggest that they represent a continuum.

The concept of a 'soft' to 'hard' continuum
This continuum might look like this:

Soft $\longleftarrow$ $\longrightarrow$ *Hard*

Reputation management	*Marketing*
Co-operative	*Competitive*
Passive	*Active*

It might be interesting for readers, firstly, to place themselves on this continuum in general terms, and secondly to position various aspects of the school such as the brochure, relationships with the media and meeting visitors. It is likely that they will not all be the same, although there may be a bias towards one side or the other.

The school's situation in respect of rising or falling rolls, the number of schools in the immediate vicinity, urban or rural, being under threat or not, personal views and professional views, are all examples of things which may affect your attitudes and hence your positioning on the continuum.

Distinction between the primary and secondary services
This is a distinction which is particularly difficult to apply to education. Firstly, 'primary' and 'secondary' are words invariably used to describe types of school, and which evoke immediate images of these in our minds. Secondly, we do not think in terms of primary and secondary services anyway.

- The **primary**, basic or first service in which schools are involved is that of educating the pupils. It could be argued that this is the *only* reason for their existence. It is the purpose for which we were trained; it may be the reason for entering and staying in the service.

- The **secondary** or additional service of schools is to respond to the demands of parents and the community at large. It is one of telling people what is going on in the school. This is an area for which few teachers have yet been trained.

An example of these two types of service might be that of an airline. The primary service is to transport people from one place to another as safely and quickly as possible. The secondary services are the comfort of the seats, the leg room, the quality of the meals and even the friendliness of the stewardesses and stewards on the planes. As all airlines, hopefully, transport you safely and quickly, it tends to be the secondary services which determine whether we travel by British Airways, Air France or any other airline.

The same idea can be applied to education. All schools provide an education for the children, and with the introduction of the National Curriculum this education will be increasingly similar. Therefore it is the additional or secondary services which are more likely to determine the choice of one school or another. As with airlines, some people may not mind which school they use as long as it is the nearest and the cheapest; others will exercise their choice by taking a long and careful look at what is on offer before deciding.

Partners in education

Some Heads and teachers will see their work as being a partnership between teacher, parent and child and that *all* of these three are part of 'the school'. They don't see the parents as 'outsiders' or 'clients' in any way at all. This is certainly true, and is one way of looking at schools. It does not seem to be at odds with reputation management where we are working *together* to improve education for all children and then sharing this, with pride, when it is done well.

Because we are working together we talk of 'our' school and 'my' school instead of 'the' school. This indicates the togetherness and family nature of the process. This is surely an excellent thing and it ought to be so in all schools. If it is *not* so, then what can be done about it?

Short term and long term

In the short term reputation management is about improvements in communication and how these are managed. In the long term by improving the reputation of schools, parents—and more importantly *politicians*—are likely to give more money and funding to education for the benefit of all those concerned.

RESEARCH INTO REPUTATION MANAGEMENT

Reputation management is the way in which Heads control the school's destiny, through acting positively, rather than reactively, in their relations with the wider society. The whole notion of *managing* the reputation of the school, rather than allowing that reputation to accrue by the haphazard impressions of those outside, is well understood by good Headteachers.

The five main elements of reputation management identified by a group of Headteachers are:

- Positive information
- Giving access
- Involvement with the community
- Public appearances
- Fostering good standards

Positive information
The Heads gave positive information to the local press and local radio. This was seen as 'free' publicity, whereas cost seemed to be a constraint on information in the brochure. Other examples of positive information included advertising, giving talks to a whole variety of groups in the local community such as the Women's Institute and Rotary, and making sure people knew where the school was.

Giving access
The Heads gave access to interested parents, to present parents and to governors. They made local residents feel that the school was a friendly place. Other areas of importance were: having an excellent 'front office', hiring out the school premises for use by local groups and ensuring tours and interviews with prospective parents were of a high quality.

Managing a school's reputation through providing access to its premises is not so much a question of how many people are allowed to pass over the threshold, but rather the quality of the welcome they receive when they do so. People are easily put off by an offhand reception; the 'first contact' with the school secretary or receptionist is vital.

Involvement with the community
This included involvement in daily events and church life by known members of the school, in *creating* local events, eg celebrating a school's anniversary in 'period' style and in charitable undertakings by pupils and staff.

Essentially, reputation management via involvement in the community in all its forms requires genuine respect for what the community has to offer; it is based on confidence that the values embodied in the school can only gain from staff and pupils' allegiance to, or involvement with, community groups.

Public appearances
Examples of public appearances are the behaviour and dress of pupils in public, especially when between sites. Although this aspect of a school's reputation is perhaps the most superficial of any listed here, it can also be the most broadly influential in conveying an impression of the school to the locality, for good or ill.

Fostering good standards

The Heads in a recent research project fostered good standards by the quality of work, evidenced within the school, neatness of uniform, care of the school by the pupils, certificates of praise for children and in letters to parents.

Many Headteachers felt that fostering good standards within the school was the most *valid* form of reputation management, if not the most *visible*. Most of the tactics related to this theme seemed to have the purpose of enhancing the self-respect of the institution, and of establishing a consensus of values between staff, pupils and parents. There was a belief that if all shared the same view of what constituted a good reputation, and worked together to create it, the rest of the world would somehow find out.

WORKING TOGETHER

There are many ways in which schools can and do work together. Some of the ways in which groups of schools, in an area or in a town, may work together are to:

- improve the continuity of the curriculum;
- improve the quality of the education which they provide;
- show how the education that they *all* provide is of a high standard;
- by *not* competing against each other for pupils.

By presenting a good image of a group of schools, a good image of education generally is presented, which might do something to offset the bad press that some feel schools and education have received recently.

Another example of working together can be demonstrated by inviting both the parents *and the child* at parents' evenings, where appropriate.

State schools, by working together, can also combat the upturn in independent schools generally, and prep schools in particular. In the past parents have often kept children in the state system until eleven and then changed. There is now a trend to start them in prep schools right from the beginning.

It might be argued that the National Curriculum, assessment, grant maintained schools, City Technology Colleges etc will make the state sector more competitive with independent schools and be much less expensive.

REPRESENTING REALITY

Reeves and Capel in 'Presenting a Primary School Image' in *Management in Education* suggest that 'communication' is the presentation of the school's image. If properly considered and planned the image will be the one which *the school* has adopted and chosen to present. If not, the perceived image will be out of the school's control and almost certainly not what is intended. Schools would do better to control their image than be controlled by it.

The image communicated to a school's publics must be a true representation of what the school is and does. Similarly, what the school is and does must truly reflect the image it has chosen to communicate. Any disparity will soon be noted by the publics and the image will then include reaction to that disparity.

CONCLUSION

If those involved in a school believe that it offers a good education, then they will want their children to receive that education. There seems little point in making available a valuable service and then not letting anybody know about it! Parents must be offered an informed choice rather than an uninformed one.

Activities

Some of the questions which have been asked in this chapter are now presented in a form which makes them easier to use as activities.

'SOFT' AND 'HARD' MARKETING CONTINUUM

The concept here is that marketing can be seen as a continuum:

SOFT ◀─────────────────────────────▶ HARD

Reputation management   *Marketing*
Co-operative   *Competitive*
Passive   *Active*

Your own outlook
In general terms, where would you put yourself on this continuum?

SOFT ◀─────────────────────────────▶ HARD

Now place your school in respect of these headings

The school prospectus or brochure

SOFT ◀─────────────────────────────▶ HARD

Relations with the media

SOFT ◀─────────────────────────────▶ HARD

Meeting visitors

SOFT ◀─────────────────────────────▶ HARD

Parents

SOFT ◀─────────────────────────────▶ HARD

The children

SOFT ◀─────────────────────────────▶ HARD

PRIMARY AND SECONDARY SERVICES

Primary services
What are the primary, basic or first services of our school?

Secondary services
What are the secondary or additional services of your school?

Now go through the lists again and underline or tick the ones that you actually do.

REPUTATION MANAGEMENT

Reputation management is the way in which you are in control of the school's destiny and act positively, rather than reactively, in relationships with the wider society.

Positive information
What are the ways in which you give positive information about the school?

Information given   *How given*

Giving access
To whom do you give access to the school?
To whom given   *How often*

Involvement with the community
Wht involvement do you have with the community?
What part of community   *Nature of involvement*

Public appearances
What public appearances do you make?
Nature of public   *Frequency/type of appearance*

Fostering good standards
What good standards do you foster in the school?
Standard   *How fostered*

Now go through the lists again
  • *underline* the ones which you think are most valid.
  • *tick* the ones which you think are the most visible.

WORKING TOGETHER

Who could work together?
List the groups that could work together.
   Groups

- Go through the list and underline or tick the ones you actually do now.
- Go through the list again and put a star beside the ones that you *could* do and that you would like to do in the future.

What could they do?
What kind of activities *could* you do together?
   Activity   *Benefits*

- Go through the list and underline or tick the ones you actually do now.
- Go through the list again and put a star beside the ones that you *could* do and that you would like to do in the future.

3
Marketing the School

In this chapter we will take an overview of the whole marketing process. Each stage will be considered in turn. This will be done in some detail and it is intended to take a practical approach towards the marketing of the school. To help the reader achieve the right kind of marketing for their own school there will be many questions to consider. Inevitably, some will be more appropriate than others depending on the school, the locality and also how much marketing has been done in the past. Nevertheless the reader is encouraged *to go through the whole process* and not to skip any of the stages, despite any temptation to do so!

THE MARKETING CYCLE

Marketing is not merely 'selling'; it involves a series of activities which must be done in the right order if the whole is to be successful. These activities can be listed in order:

- **Developing a team**.
  Who can I get to help?

- **The marketing environment.**
  What is the general situation as far as my school is concerned?

- **The marketing audit.**
  What is the specific situation as far as my school is concerned?

- **Producing a marketing plan**.
  Marketing strategy – what do we want to do about it?
  Marketing objectives – how are we going to set about them?
  Marketing plan – what are our Action Plans?

- **Marketing implementation.**
  Doing it!

- **Marketing evaluation**.
  How did we get on?

The process of marketing is cyclic or spiral (as opposed to linear) in nature for the marketing evaluation items link strongly with the marketing audit. This is shown in diagrammatic form in figure 3.1.

Figure 3.1 The marketing cycle

These items have been expanded into:

A detailed marketing cycle

- **Developing a team**

- **The market environment** (the Context for the Audit)
  The aims and values of the school
  Policies and initiatives from central government and the LEA
  Trends, changes in parents' attitudes
  Recent or anticipated competitor actions
  Other views and perspectives

- **Marketing audit** (the Content of the Audit)
  Comprehensive
  Systematic
  Objective
  Periodic

Market research
Collection of information
SWOT plus PAC
DEN
Analysis of the information

- **Production of a Marketing Plan**

Marketing strategy
Definition of aims
To whom is the campaign directed?
What methods are going to be used?
Resources
Time

Marketing objectives
Developing objectives
Establishing priorities

Marketing programmes
Production of Action Plans and their approval

- **Marketing implementation**
Communication
Written documents
Face to face communications
Internal markets
External markets
Meeting the Customers
Brochures
The Media

- **Marketing evaluation**

Quality control
Performance Indicators
Questionnaires to parents

The first of these, Developing a Team, will be considered now. Each of the other headings will be considered in later chapters.

DEVELOPING A TEAM

Neither the management nor the actual marketing of the school can be done by one person. It is the kind of task that needs a small *team* of people to work together. There are two reasons for this:

- The first is that by sharing out the various tasks amongst a group it will lighten the load on any one person.

- The second is that by having a group there is likely to be a widening of ideas, expertise and viewpoints.

It is suggested that a senior member of staff should be responsible for the managing of the marketing of the school. This may or may not be the Headteacher; it certainly should be somebody who has influence within the school and is interested in doing the task. This person should work closely with the Head.

The small team should include governors, parents and teachers with the relevant expertise or interest. The first, of many, activities is to list those people who *could* help, together with what they have to offer. Try to be as creative and divergent in your thinking to include as many people as possible from outside as well as inside the school. Having listed the possible people, the next stage is to choose those who are most likely to build into the right team.

Having built the team, it is suggested each of the elements in the cycle should be taken in turn.

Activities

Some of the questions which have been asked in this chapter are now presented in a form which may make them easier to use as an activity.

DEVELOPING A TEAM

Which individual should be responsible for overall marketing of your school?

Name   *Why?*

List those people who *could* help

Staff   *What each can offer*

_____   _____

_____   _____

_____   _____

_____   _____

Governors

_____   _____

_____   _____

_____   _____

_____   _____

Parents

_____   _____

_____   _____

_____   _____

_____   _____

Others

_____   _____

_____   _____

_____   _____

_____   _____

4
The Market Environment

THE CONTEXT FOR THE AUDIT

The marketing of the school, its planning and implementation, needs to be set within:

- The aims and values of the school
- Policies and initiatives from central government and the LEA
- Trends and changes in parent attitudes
- Recent or anticipated competitor actions
- Other views and perspectives

Wherever possible both *quantitative* and *qualitative* information should be accumulated. Quantitative information is that which can be counted, added up and measured; qualitative information is that which cannot be counted, but is valuable because it contains feelings about the situation.

THE AIMS AND VALUES OF THE SCHOOL

The marketing of the school needs to be set within the aims and values of the school as a whole and not considered in isolation. These aims and values may already have been written down in a form which can be used in this context. If not, it may be necessary to start by devising a **mission statement** of what the school *does* aim to do. The advantage of a school mission statement is that *everything* which happens within the school can then be aimed at achieving this purpose. Certainly the marketing of the school should reflect the values of the school as a whole. For example, if the school sees itself as an academic institution, with strict discipline and uniform, the marketing should reflect this not only in its content, but also its style. In contrast the school may be one which prides itself on being a caring, relaxed place where learning is only one part of the experience of the children. In this case the marketing of the school will be totally different. The marketing plan needs to be a part of the whole School Development Plan, not separate from it.

POLICIES AND INITIATIVES FROM CENTRAL GOVERNMENT AND THE LEA

Government policies such as the National Curriculum and its assessment and LEA policies on open enrolment cannot be ignored. Questions which ought to be asked are, for example:

- Which are the most important for your particular school?
- How does the school fit in to the national scene and that of the local Education Authority?
- Is there a new housing estate being built nearby?
- Is a new school being built?
- What are the trends in population, both in general and also that of school age?

The school cannot isolate itself from what is happening in the rest of the area. It needs to consider not only how this is affecting the school now, but also in the near future, say the next year, and further ahead in three to five years' time.

TRENDS, CHANGES IN PARENT ATTITUDES

Again the questions that need asking are:

- What are the trends in the area concerning all the schools?
- Are these trends easy or difficult to change?
- Which of these trends *can* you change? Which cannot be changed and so are not worth the time and effort attempting to do so?

The answers to these questions concerning the trends in your area must be considered before you move on to what you might do as an individual school in the next part of the cycle.

The changes in parent attitudes which are important in your area have to be noted. For example, are the parent attitudes changing towards or away from state education in your area? Perhaps this is something on which you could work collectively with other schools near you with a view to change, as it may be too large a project to be considered on your own.

RECENT OR ANTICIPATED COMPETITOR ACTIONS

Once more, it is important to find out what other schools in your area are doing. If you started marketing your school now, would you be in the lead? Or is the converse true—everybody else is well on the way, and you have to catch up? Can you afford *not* to market your school when everybody else is doing so? As before, consider not only what is happening now, but also what might happen in the near and distant future.

OTHER VIEWS AND PERSPECTIVES

What other views might be taken into consideration? What are the views of the governors, parents, teachers, pupils and local residents, on all of the above points? This will be considered in rather more detail in the next chapter.

Activities

Some of the questions which have been asked in this chapter are now presented in a form which may make them easier to use as activities.

THE AIMS AND VALUES OF THE SCHOOL

What are the main aims of the school?

Aim   *Why important*

What are the values which the school thinks are important?

Value   *Why considered important*

Mission statement
Devise a Mission Statement for the school.
A clear Mission Statement ought to be able to state the main aims and purposes of the school in no more than 25 words. Ideally this is a group activity for all the staff:

_____

_____

_____

_____

_____

_____

_____

MARKET ENVIRONMENT: The Context for the Audit

What are the main policies and initiatives from central government which you are trying to adopt at the present time?

Policy or initiative   *Reason for response*

What are the main policies and initiatives from the LEA which you are trying to adopt at the present time?

Policy or initiative   *Reason for adopting*

What are the trends in your area which you need to consider?

Trend   *Why important*

- Go through this list and put a star beside those about which you can do nothing.

What are the changes in parent attitudes which are important in your area?

Change in attitude   *Why important*

What are the recent or anticipated actions being made by your competitors?

Action   *Likely impact on your school*

What other views and perspectives need to be considered in your school?

View   *Why relevant*

5
Marketing Audit

The previous chapter was concerned with the context for the audit, the market environment; this chapter is intended to answer the question, 'What is the situation here?' It is concerned with market research: the collection and analysis of information.

REQUIREMENTS FOR A MARKETING AUDIT

A marketing audit needs to be:

- Comprehensive
- Systematic
- Objective
- Periodic

Comprehensive
The marketing audit needs to cover the whole of the organisation, not just those areas which are causing concern. It should be wide ranging in the areas investigated, not narrow and inward looking.

Systematic
The marketing audit should be systematic. In later sections this systematic process will be explained and a variety of activities outlined.

Objective
It is all too easy to make the marketing audit a cosy, self-congratulating process. It should be as rigorous and objective as possible and involve governors, parents and others from outside the school as they can help objectivity.

Periodic
Although many schools may be undertaking the marketing audit for the first time it is suggested that this is not a 'one off', but a regular,

repeated activity. It needs to be updated annually, or certainly bi-annually, as it is easy for the information to get out of date. It should be part of an overall plan and not completed only when something untoward crops up.

MARKET RESEARCH

The mere collection of information does not ensure a client-centred approach. Two stages of activity need to be involved in market research.

- Collection of information
- Analysis of information

COLLECTION OF INFORMATION

What follows is a series of practical activities for the collection of information. As many as possible should be completed.

How well known is your school?
All those in schools tend to assume that because they are so involved with the school everybody else has similar views. The question to ask is, how well known is your school in the immediate vicinity? Ask a member of staff, parent or governor—preferably somebody who is not well known in the locality—to go to a bus stop or to some other convenient assembly point a quarter to half a mile away from the school; get them to ask 20 different people at 20 different times for directions to the school, and record the results. Do people know where your school is? Do they know if it is a primary or secondary school? Is it a school for boys or girls or both? What are the ages of the children? It is not unusual to find that people within a stone's throw of the school are blissfully unaware of its existence or have only a hazy idea of its purpose. Of course this may be seen as a positive factor because it may mean the children are well behaved on the way home. On the other hand it may mean that the school is not as well known as you might like.

Define your catchment area
Define not only your 'official' catchment area, but the *actual* area from which your pupils come. Do you *know* where the pupils come from in a detailed way? How many pupils are from 'out of area'?

Rather more difficult to find out, perhaps, is how many children who are in your official area are going to other schools and the reasons for this choice. The purpose for acquiring this knowledge is that, with limited time and resources, it is prudent to concentrate on efforts in the areas where it may have the most effect.

Discover how parents of pupils hear about the school
Information to gather here would be:

- How did the parents of the children at your school find out about the school in the first place?
- Have they always lived in the area?
- Was it by talking to neighbours or other parents, from the estate agent or reading about the school in the newspaper?

Every school secretary, or whoever answers the telephone, could and should be trained to ask each prospective parent who rings up the school how they heard about the school in the first place. This question should be put on any forms which new parents have to fill in. If there is no previous record, new parents should be asked for this information when they come to visit the school for the first time.

If there is no record of how parents heard about your school, and you wish to build up this data, one way to find out is by sending a **questionnaire** to all the parents of your first and second year pupils: ask them how they found out about the school and why they decided to send their children to your school rather than others in the locality. This questionnaire could be sent separately or as part of a newsletter.

Other ways of collecting this information are:

- by a **telephone poll**, where a number of parents are telephoned to find out the answers.

- by a **meeting with a sample** of parents or representatives of the community. This might be at a parents' evening or a governors' meeting, for example.

Identifying parents' needs
In order to indentify the parents' needs, expectations, hopes and desires for their children it may be necessary to ask them either formally or informally. The *answers* to these qustions are market research, but this information may also be seen as 'quality control'. This indicates the cyclic or spiral nature of marketing as opposed to a linear approach. Neverthless it might help to meet the needs of the

parents if you *know* what these are as opposed to *thinking* you understand them.

Identifying the pupils' needs

Are the pupils' needs identical to those of the parents? If not how are they similar or different? Throughout this book parent and child are treated as one unit, as explained in Chapter 1. Nevertheless, the pupils may have interests which differ from those of the parents, and which should be met by the school management.

What image does your school have?

The images of the school in the eyes of the children and parents, the local community, the governors and the staff may not be the same. This might, therefore, be another area where it is necessary to ask each of these groups separately. It may also be worth trying to differentiate between the *image* of the school and 'reality'. One method of obtaining a differing view of the school is to go into the nearest estate agents, pretend you are moving in to the area and are a prospective 'new parent' and ask *them* to tell you about the school.

What factors are important in determining the 'public image' of the school?

Once more this might be more successful if it combines the views of all concerned with the school. The staff and their attitudes are likely to be major factors in determining the public image of the school. How the staff dress, their punctuality, whether they smoke, the time they leave school in the evenings, how they greet and talk to the parents and pupils are all examples of ways in which the staff determine the public image of the school.

SWOT

The SWOT technique is most useful in examining the Strengths, Weaknesses, Opportunities and Threats to the school. In essence it involves asking a series of questions and, more importantly, working together to provide some answers in this development stage of the marketing cycle. Some of the questions which might be asked are:

Strengths
What are the strongest points about the school?
How widely are they known?
What is done to promote them?

Weaknesses
What are the weaknesses? Be as honest as you can!
What can be done to remedy them?

Opportunities
What opportunities are there to 'sell' the school?
Are they taken?
What about the *timing* of these new opportunities?

Threats
What are the potential threats to the school?
Don't procrastinate – act!

It is better to concentrate first of all on the positive aspects of the school. Try to emphasise the strengths and the opportunities rather than the negative side of the weaknesses and threats. This is often an attitude of mind or a way of looking at things. For example if the numbers in the school are decreasing and class sizes falling, do not see this as negative; rather, see it as a strength because there are small classes and children can be given more individual attention.

PAC
In addition to the Strengths, Weaknesses, Opportunities and Threats there should be added Performance, Actual conditions, Capabilities.

Performance
What has been the performance in the past?
Areas that might be considered are academic, sporting, musical and social.

Actual conditions
What are the actual conditions to consider when looking at the school?
What are the 'Ah, but...' questions?
For example, 'Ah, remember we are still a selective area for secondary education.'

Capabilities
What are the capabilities of the parents, governors and staff?
List the capabilities of individual staff, parents and governors.

Distinctive Educational Niche (DEN) or Unique Selling Point (USP)
Having completed the above section it is well worth developing a Unique Selling Point (USP), or an adaptation, the Distinctive Educational Niche (DEN).

What is **distinctive** about our school?

- What makes our lessons in this school distinctive?
- What makes our school distinctive?
- What is our 'trade mark'?

The idea may also be applied to a group of schools:

- What makes our pyramid distinctive?
- How are the schools in this town distinctive?

By developing this concept of distinctiveness, it may be possible for schools to develop their strengths into something distinctive or unique.

The second element of the DEN is **educational**. The main purpose of schools is the education of pupils. It is easy to forget this when looking at marketing and the management tasks involved.

The third element is that of the **niche**. It needs to be recognised that we cannot appeal to all of the people all of the time; it might be more realistic to aim at *some* of the people all of the time. This is a niche market as opposed to the whole market.

A whole series of DENs need to be built up. There should be a number of ways in which your school is distinctive and which will appeal to different people in different ways. What are required are multiple lists of excellence.

The question of 'How do we *show* excellence?' will be considered in later chapters of this book.

ANALYSIS OF INFORMATION

The educational world is full of data which have been collected and never put to use. Analysis is a time-consuming and potentially expensive activity. It can be carried out most effectively, and cheaply, if the analysis stage is considered and thought through before the information is collected. Approximate costings are available. For example, using computer analysis and employing an external agency or existing school staff to carry out data input will cost 10-20 pence per 30 item questionnaire, with the costs of reproducing and reporting the information to be added to this.

Unprocessed data are of little value to management or teachers. A simple look through a set of questionnaires will not suffice. Properly analysed, the information must be fed back to teaching and management staff as appropriate.

It is not intended to go into detail about the analysis of information, but some of the following points might be considered.

Quantitative data
Production of:
- tally charts
- graphs: column, line or pie as appropriate
- tables of information

Qualitative data
This is often better handled using a word processor. It might include:

- typing in of raw data
- collecting similar comments together under appropriate headings
- re-ordering the comments within these headings
- making a synopsis of the comments
- listing the main points made

The key role for professional staff in such a marketing approach is in bridging the gap between **information** and the **action** which results from it. How to achieve this action will be considered in later chapters. Staff should not merely *react* to the views expressed and automatically make changes suggested by the parents, children or anybody else. School teaching and management staff must *interpret* the information produced by the above stages and make professional decisions which are best for school and client in the short, medium and long term. It is on their own judgement that they must ultimately rely.

Activities

Some of the questions which have been asked in this chapter are now presented in a form which may make them easier to use as activities.

MARKET RESEARCH

How well known is your school?
Ask a member of staff, parent or governor, preferably somebody not well known in the locality, to go to a bus stop or some other convenient assembly point a quarter to half a mile away from the school and ask 20 different people at 20 different times for directions and general information about the school.

Question   *No. out of 20 correct*

Do people know where your school is?   _____

Do they know if it is a primary or a
   secondary school?   _____

Is it a school for boys or girls or both?   _____

What are the ages of the children?   _____

- It is not unusual to find that people within a stone's throw of the school are blissfully unaware of its existence or have only a hazy idea of its purpose.

What is your catchment area?
What is the 'official' catchment area of the school?

What is the *actual* area from which your pupils come?

How many pupils are from 'out of area'?

How many children in your official area are going to other schools?

What are the reasons for their choice?

Do you *know* where the pupils come from, not in vague terms, but in detail? If not *find out!*

How do parents hear about the school?
How did the parents of the children at your school find out about the
school in the first place?

Have they always lived in the area?

Was it by talking to neighbours or other parents?

Does the school secretary ask?

Is the question on any new parent forms?

Are they asked at new parent interviews?

- If you have no record of how parents heard about your school,
  one idea might be to **send a questionnaire to all parents of first
  and second year pupils** to ask them.

What are the parents' needs?
What do the parents need of the school?

Need   *How important to them*

What are the parents' expectations for their children at your school?

Expectation   *How important to them*

What are the parents' hopes and desires for their children at your school?

What are the pupils' needs?
What are the pupils' needs, expectations, hopes and desires of the school?

Need   *How important to them*

How does this vary from that of the parents?

What image does your school have?
Write down four key words which you think would describe the
school from the *children's* point of view:

_____   _____

_____   _____

Write down four key words which you think would describe the
school from the *parents'* point of view:

_____   _____

_____   _____

- Having written down what *you* think, now go and ask the pupils
  and parents what *they* think!

What factors do you think are important in determining the 'public
face' of your school? (List the factors, then rate them on a scale of 1-5
where 5 means that you deal well with this factor and 1 means that
nothing is done).

Factors   *Rating*

- Having written down what *you* think, now go and ask the staff
  what *they* think.

Go into the nearest Estate Agents to your school, pretend you are
moving in to the area and are a prospective 'new parent'. Ask *them* to
rate your school.

SWOT

Strengths

What are the strongest points about your school?

How widely are they known?

What is done to promote them?

Weaknesses

What are the weaknesses? Be as honest as you can!

What can be done to remedy them?

Opportunities

What opportunities are there to 'sell' the school?

Are they taken?

What about the *timing* of these new opportunities?

Threats

What are the potential threats to the school?

What can you do about them?

PAC

Performance
What has been the performance in the recent past?

Aspect of performance   *Level of performance*

Actual conditions
What are the actual conditions which need to be considered when looking at the school? What are the 'Ah, but...' questions?

Capabilities
What are the particular capabilities of members of staff which *could* be used to the benefit of the school?

Name   *Capability*

What are the particular capabilities of members of the governing body?

Name   *Capability*

What are the particular capabilities of individual parents?

Name   *Capability*

DISTINCTIVE EDUCATIONAL NICHE (DEN)

What is distinctive about our school?

What makes our school *distinctive*?

What is our 'trade mark'?

Which niches are we aiming at?

What separate groups of parents *could* we aim at?

Group   *Reason for targeting*

What are your school's 'DENs'?
A 'DEN' has something which is distinctive about your school. At which section of the parent population is it aimed?

Distinctive factor   *Targeted parents*

How do we show this distinctiveness?

In general ways   *In specific ways*

COST OF COLLECTING INFORMATION

In order to assist in the collection of data, it usually helps to decide exactly what data you require and how costly it might be to find. That is what this matrix is designed to do.

Column 1	Column 2	Column 3	Column 4	Column 5
Questions	Information required	Likely sources of information	Accessibility of information	Cost of information

Some of the questions mentioned previously may be put in column 1. Having completed that column, complete the others.

Column 4 is scored   0 = not available
                  1 = access very difficult
                  2 = needs some effort
                  3 = readily available

Column 5 is scored   1 = very expensive
                  2 = significant costs
                  3 = low/no costs

This information may be summarised on one sheet:

Questions	Information Inaccessible and costly	Information Inaccessible not costly	Information Accessible and costly	Information Accessible not costly	Recommendations

6
Producing a Marketing Plan

This chapter will explain how to produce a marketing plan. It will involve:

- **Marketing strategy**
  Definition of aims
  To whom is the campaign directed?
  What methods are going to be used?
  Resources
  Time

- **Marketing objectives**
  Developing objectives
  Establishing priorities

- **Marketing programmes**
  Production of Action plans and their approval

MARKETING STRATEGY

Definition of aims
Our first task is to decide what it is we are trying to achieve. Marketing aims are likely to be 'global' terms. What is the desired outcome of the whole public relations effort? It could be ongoing and comprehensive, for example to renew public confidence in the state school system; or it could be to increase the number of children enrolling at this school. More specifically it could be to increase the school's coverage in the local paper or to get its name mentioned on television. There is likely to be a whole series of aims.

To whom is the campaign directed?
There are many publics in the school's community. The same message won't necessarily have the same effect on each audience, so it must be tailored to fit each group's viewpoint and perceptions.

Identify what each of these publics needs to understand for the school to be successful and concentrate on this.

What methods are going to be used?
Identify communications channels or activities that could be used to communicate the messages. You may wish to consider newsletters, the news media, open house and so on. Some of these may already be used; some may be new to your school.

Resources
Marketing strategy will need to include thought about the resources which are *needed* and, perhaps more important, those which are *available*. One of the problems here may be that there is no precedent for the use of resources in this fashion. There may never have been a budget for marketing in the past, so it may be difficult to set one in the future. All those involved in managing the school will probably want a say in deciding the budget for marketing. Many feel that all the resources available to the school should be spent on the pupils directly and that marketing is a peripheral activity.

Marketing may be an area where a school needs to spend money to gain money: each pupil attracted to the school who would not have otherwise have attended is worth in the region of £1,000. Another view is that you may not be able to afford *not* to spend resources in this manner if all other schools are doing so. Quality products such as brochures say a great deal about the school—poor quality brochures and newsletters can say even more!

Time
Time is a resource worth considering here, not only from the point of view of the time which it is *desirable* to spend on marketing, but also the time which the head, staff and parents are *prepared* to spend on marketing. The two may not be the same.

• What is the time-frame of your marketing programme?
• What is the plan for this year, this term?

Having decided what you wish to do in broad terms, and in principle, you can now come to a more detailed stage.

MARKETING OBJECTIVES

Developing objectives

Once communications activities are selected, determine the objectives to be accomplished. Objectives should be **SMART**:

Specific
Measurable
Achievable
Realistic
Time constrained

- Specific means making the objectives as precise as possible and not being 'woolly'.

- Objectives should be measurable, so that everyone knows when they have been reached. This is probably the most important and also the most problematic as much of education is difficult to measure.

- Objectives should be achievable or attainable, or all concerned will become discouraged. On the other hand they need to be challenging so that they will give people something to aim for.

- If the objectives are not realistic, and seen to be so by those concerned, they will once again be discouraged.

- Finally if there are no deadlines nobody will know by when the objectives are supposed to be achieved.

These objectives should be decided in conjunction with staff, parents, governors and also the LEA if appropriate. Differing tactics may need to be employed with these very different groups in order to reach a marketing consensus.

Establishing priorities

Having decided on the objectives, they need to be prioritised. The staff in particular should have a major role to play here; they will probably be the main people involved in carrying out any scheme. Everybody should now know what they are trying to achieve and should work single-mindedly towards success.

MARKETING PROGRAMMES

Production of action plans

An action plan should include:

- **who** should do **what** by **when**

There should be a **named person** to complete a **specific activity** within an agreed **time**. The action plan will give a detailed schedule of what is to be completed this term, this month and this week (as opposed to this year!).

It is important to progress through the stages of strategy, objectives and action plan. They *are* separate stages, in which the first is concerned with general principles, the second with the tactics, and the third with all the detail. Each of the first two stages will need consultation with staff and governors before they are made public.

The final stage is to obtain the resources needed and get the programme underway, making frequent checks to be sure the approach is on the right track.

SUMMARY

In summary, then, a marketing plan must:

- Explain the **situation,** both present and future.

- Specify **results** that are expected.

- Identify the **resources** that will be needed to carry out the planned actions.

- Describe the **actions** that are to take place and who is responsible for implementing them.

- Permit **monitoring** of actions and results.

Activities

Some of the questions discussed in this chapter are now presented in a form which may make them easier to use as activities for the production of a Marketing Plan.

MARKETING STRATEGY

Definition of aims

1. What is the desired outcome of the whole public relations effort?

2. What do we plan to do this year?

Action   *Reason*

3. What do we plan to do this term?

Action   *Reason*

4. To whom is our campaign directed?

Target group   *Why targeted*

5. What methods are we going to use?

Method   *Why selected*

6. What resources are needed?

Resource   *Why needed*

7. What resources are available?

Resource   *Availability*

8. What time is it desirable to spend?

Amount of time   *Why desirable*

9. How much time are we prepared to spend?

Amount of time   *Limiting factors*

MARKETING OBJECTIVES

Objectives should be SMART

- Specific
- Measurable (the most important point)
- Achievable
- Realistic
- Time constrained

Developing objectives
What are our objectives for this **year**?

What are our objectives for this **term**?

What are our objectives for this **month**?

What are our objectives for this **week**?

- Establish priorities. What are *your* priorities? Take another careful look at your objectives, and then number them in order of priority.

MARKETING PROGRAMMES

An Action Plan should include:

- **Who** should do **what** by **when**

Production of Action Plans
This will be a detailed schedule of what is to be completed.
NAMED PERSON to complete a SPECIFIC ACTIVITY within an agreed TIME

Named person	*Specific activity*	*Agreed time*

In summary then a marketing plan must:

- Explain the **situation,** both present and future.
- Specify **results** that are expected.
- Identify the **resources** that will be needed to carry out the planned actions.
- Describe the **actions** that are to take place and who is responsible for implementing them.
- Permit **monitoring** of actions and results.

7
Marketing Implementation

This section of the marketing cycle is concerned with **Communicating** to our market. We have analysed the market environment, conducted a marketing audit and produced a marketing plan; it is now time to stop the talking and put it all into action. The communication will normally be in the form of:

- **Written documents**, or
- **Face to face communications.**

The second of these will probably be more effective in changing people's views about the school and education in general and yet much of the effort in schools seems to be on the former. In this section, both will be considered.

INTERNAL COMMUNICATIONS

Any discussion of communication generally turns to external publics. Internal communication, however, often creates the greatest problems and suffers the greatest neglect. The school should first organise an effective *internal* communications programme because:

- The school will never reach its goals unless all those involved with the school really understand what the goals are.

- Everybody needs to know their own individual roles in helping reach these goals.

- Members of the school feel a greater sense of ownership when they *are* personally involved.

- Members of staff, both teaching and non-teaching, have knowledge and skills that can be tapped to make the school more effective. Working in partnership can lead to real teamwork, where the staff as a whole becomes more effective than the sum of its individual parts.

- The right hand must know what the left hand is doing.

Considering that face-to-face communication is most influential, the broad range of personal contacts made by the many staff members can have an immense impact on a school's image. To the general public, every person who works in the school is considered authoritative. Whether the next door neighbour is a Headteacher or a school cleaner, what he or she says about the educational system can carry a lot of weight.

It makes sense for the Head to consider every member of the staff, both teaching and non-teaching, that is *all* those who work in the school, as important members of the public relations team. They should be kept informed of all the major issues facing the school – not just those in their specific area of responsibility; they should be made to feel that they are a valued part of the school 'family'. The importance of cultivating that 'family feeling' cannot be overstated, and its impact can be greater than just a public relations tool. Open, honest two-way communication is the bulwark of high morale and the key to motivated staff. A sense of community results from the sharing of common information, common feelings, and common goals. That sense of community can exist within the staff when all feel informed, when they feel involved and when they feel their ideas are heard.

All of the above is also true for the governors, parents and pupils. All are ambassadors of the school and *can* help if:

- they **realise they are ambassadors**. It is up to those concerned with marketing the school to ensure that everybody *does* realise this. It should be in the forefront of everybody's minds if the marketing of the school is to be successful.

- All these ambassadors need to be **kept informed** about all the good things which are happening in the school so that they can tell the public at large.

EXTERNAL COMMUNICATIONS

A number of the external markets of schools can be listed. Some of them are obvious (eg parents), others may not have been seen as markets of the school in the past (eg local organisations). Comments can be made under each of the following headings with some ideas about what can be achieved with each. They are in A-Z order for easy reference.

Brass band, choirs etc

Many schools have a brass band, choir, country dance group, gymnastics team and so on, which can, and do, 'represent' the school at local functions. These functions range from the official parade through the streets to the playing or singing for the local old age pensioners at Christmas time. All of these show the school in a good light and pupils, staff and parents working together for the wider community. What could *your* school do in this way?

Churches

The various local churches have congregations who may well be interested in what is happening to the school. This is not only true for Church Aided or Controlled schools, but also for County schools. The church hall, where many people meet, is often the centre of a village community; it could be an ideal place to display children's work.

Citizens' Advice Bureaux

From enquiries received by the National Independent Schools Information Service these bureaux appear to be one of the most popular reference points for parents anxious to find out about schools in their area. It is suggested, therefore, that schools make sure the local bureaux are kept supplied with the school prospectus. A personal visit to offices in your area is likely to be more beneficial than merely sending them printed information.

Estate agents

Try to establish contacts with a representative of all the estate agents in your catchment area. Looking for a school often goes hand in hand with looking for a house in a particular area, which is why estate agents should welcome an approach from your school. Use any contacts you have with estate agents through the parents of the children at your school. Make sure that co-operative estate agents are kept supplied with as many prospectuses as they require.

Feeder schools

These are one of the obvious points to concentrate on. Make a list of the feeder schools in your catchment area from the nursery and pre-school play groups (official *and* unofficial). Invite heads or representatives of those schools or groups to visit your school. Invite them to open days, school plays, harvest festival: to whatever you do that is appropriate. Volunteer the use of your school as a venue for regional and district meetings. Make sure that visitors are shown round the school. Above all keep those feeder schools which send you pupils in touch with those pupils' later successes. The Heads and other teachers will be interested to know that 'their' pupils have settled in well, and what they are now doing. Send them the school magazine or other publications, such as newsletters.

Local industry
The personnel departments are the key points of contact. If you read in the local press of a firm moving into the school's catchment area, contact the Head of Personnel and invite him or her to visit your school for a guided tour.

Non-parents
Many of those who live near the school or in the community are *not* parents. What are you doing to market education, state education, and your school in particular for these people? They are certainly going to be voters, who can influence the funds for education! District and County Councillors and even Members of Parliament may come into this group; what are you doing to cultivate them?

Open Days
Open Days need not be designed just for the parents of existing pupils. The most successful are those where existing parents are asked in a personal letter from the Head to bring along any friends who would like to see the school at work. Personal invitations should be sent also to local dignitaries such as the Mayor, Chairman of the Chamber of Commerce, local MPs, Councillors, proprietors and editors of the local newspapers, local business people and individuals who have helped the school. A traditional form of the Open Day is a tour of empty classrooms in which there are static displays of work, often in the evening. It is much better for visitors to see pupils actually at work in their classrooms and for the Open Day to be designed, as far as possible, to show a 'normal' school working day. There should be some special attractions for the visitors to see in each of the classrooms as well as general musical or sporting activities. If Open Days are combined with spring fairs or summer fêtes they may attract sections of the community who do not normally visit the school.

Public libraries
Often public libraries, particularly the children's section, are looking
for displays of children's work. Do you ask the librarian to visit your
school with books and to help the children? Ask if they are interested
in having a copy of your school's prospectus in their reference section.

School minibus
The school minibus *can* be a good advertisement for the school if the
children who travel in it are well-behaved and a credit to the school.
The converse can also be true! The idea of pupils being ambassadors
of the school has been mentioned elsewhere in this section; it cannot
be over-emphasised. The minibus needs to be smart looking, well
maintained and painted with the name of the school along the side
and back.

Use of school buildings
The more schools can open their buildings and sports grounds to the
public, the more widely they will become known throughout the
community. Some possible suggestions are:

● open your buildings for renting after school hours;

● offer the use of school grounds for charity functions such as
  fêtes and garden parties;

● invite the local women's institutes, townswomen's guilds etc to
  use your school's premises for their meetings from time to time;

● encourage local services to use the school for art shows,
  handicraft exhibitions, concerts and other cultural activities;

● invite members of the public in to lessons in the new technology.
  Put your computer at the disposal of groups and societies.

Waiting rooms
Think of all the waiting rooms and reception areas where parents who
might be interested in sending their children to your school are sitting
doing nothing and looking for something to read: doctors' and
dentists' waiting rooms, health clinics, hospitals, hairdressers, hotels,
banks and building societies for example. These are all areas where
there could be a display of the children's work with the name of the
school included, and people will have time to admire the high quality
of the work. Look through the occupations of the parents of children

at your school to see if they can help by putting up-to-date prospectuses in the public view.

Welcome-to-the-area organisations and removal firms.
Some areas, particularly villages, have organisations, both official and unofficial, which help newcomers. Many towns have tourist and information centres. Make sure that those who run these centres know about your school. Make sure that all the local removal firms have a copy of your prospectus. Removal firms sometimes have a 'check list' for home movers which includes a section on 'schools in the area'; make sure *yours* is included.

Finally, say 'thank you'
If you discover that your school has been recommended by someone do make sure to thank the person responsible and invite him or her to visit the school. Saying 'thank you' does cost a little time, but as well as being polite, is yet another (marketing) opportunity for showing how caring the school is.

Activities

INTERNAL COMMUNICATIONS

How can your school achieve improved internal communications?

Inter-personal communications

Topic to be communicated   *Place/frequency*

Written communications

Topic to be communicated   *Method/frequency*

Problem areas in existing communications

Nature of problem   *Possible solution*

EXTERNAL COMMUNICATIONS

Parents

Purpose of communication   *Method/frequency*

Local secondary schools

Name of school   *Method/frequency of communication*

Local feeder schools

Name of school   *Method/frequency of communication*

Religious organisations

Name of organisation   *Method/frequency of communication*

Community organisations

Name of organisation   *Method/frequency of communication*

The local media

Name of newspaper etc   *Method/frequency of communication*

Local professional offices/waiting rooms

Firm   *Method/frequency of communication*

Other external markets

Description   *Method/frequency of communication*

8
Meeting the Visitor

The next three chapters offer practical help. The first of these is 'Meeting the Visitor'. The term visitor is used here to apply to anybody visiting the school, whether as a prospective parent, a County Councillor, a colleague or one of the many people who need to be 'shown round' the school for one reason or another. These are people that you would wish to see you in the 'best light'.

Tom Peters in his book *Thriving on Chaos* suggests that:

> 'Often what counts with customers is not the big thing, but a hundred little things. Everyone has a part to play in making the small improvements that make a big impression.'

We can approach this, in a positive manner, and help to make a big impression by drawing up a checklist of the hundred small things which are so easy to forget.

In the previous chapter we discussed **external** markets. Communication here might also encompass the meeting of visitors; the Head and other teachers should go out of the school and into the community to meet as many people as possible. This will get the school noticed in a positive and personal way. One way of ensuring this is to make a checklist of the external markets of the school and keep a note of when they were last contacted. It is easy to say that we are 'always' talking to groups outside school only to find that in reality the last time we did so was five years ago!

Most of what follows, however, concerns meeting those who come into the school. Its application and relevance will vary widely according to the type, size and location of the school and the experience of the Headteacher. The independent schools are well practised in this type of activity and their *Good Communications Guide* is very helpful.

FIRST IMPRESSIONS COUNT

Remember that you can only make a first impression once!

- Can your school be easily found?
- Can the way in be found?

School notices and signs
Is your school properly signposted? Are there enough signs warning motorists that they are approaching it? There should be large notice boards with the name of the school proudly displayed in large lettering. The signs should not end at the gate. There should be enough signs in the grounds to enable visitors to find their way round. For example, is the entrance to the school signposted—or do half *your* visitors end up in the kitchens or by the dustbins?

Maps and guides
Try to make sure that your school is marked on street maps, area maps or guides which any newcomer to the area might obtain. Although it may be more difficult with general commercial guides, estate agents who produce special maps can probably be persuaded to include your school on them.

The telephone directory
Make sure there is a number for parents to contact in the local telephone directory. Are there arrangements for answering the telephone *at all times* during the day, including lunchtime and in the afternoon? How do you cope with the times when the secretary is not there? Could this be improved? What about weekends and the holidays? An answering machine can help, but it needs to be monitored regularly and certainly before the end of school each day.

The Headteacher
The Headteacher must *look* the part of a professional by being smart and well-dressed as well as *being* the part. Indeed, this is true not only for the Head, but for *all* the staff. The school secretaries should go out of their way to be pleasant and to put visitors at ease, even when they are working under pressure. They could take this first meeting as an opportunity of finding out how parents first found out about the school. The entrance hall should be well lit, with children's work on the walls to create a welcoming atmosphere.

- **Try to appear efficient.** The Head's room will be visited by nearly all those who come to the school, so it should be tidy at all times. This is easier said than done, especially just before the school fête or jumble sale. Try to keep your desk neat and businesslike, with details of the visitor close to hand. An inability to find things on your desk will create an unfavourable impression. Allow the odd interruption from a pupil or a member of staff, so that the visitors will see that you are hard working and prepared to devote time to children and staff; but prevent constant interruptions.

- **The Head should interview visitors personally** if at all possible. In some larger schools it may be the Deputy head or the Head of the Infant Department who are mainly concerned with the admission of pupils. Prospective parents will still expect to see the Head at some time during their visit.

- **Sell yourself.** The parent must have confidence in the Head *personally* before s/he decides to entrust their child to the school for some of the most formative years of his or her life. Smile, be welcoming, be open, be approachable, be confident in both yourself and the school.

- **Talk about the child** and the *benefits* to the child which will come from attending your school. This is the secret of all such successful interviews. The child, whether s/he is present or not, is the most important person under discussion. Show an obvious interest in what the child has done, and in what the parents want the child to do in the future, even if they are telling you about a five year old going to Oxbridge. Show you are interested and enthusiastic about the child coming to your school, and how once s/he is there, s/he will be happy and treated as an individual.

- **Emphasise the strengths of your school** which might make it particularly suitable for their child. A professional will not be drawn into criticising or giving an adverse opinion about other schools. You may hear comments on the schools which parents have visited, or where their children attend, which are anything but complimentary. Try to turn the conversation back to talking about your own school wherever possible.

- **Put the visitors at their ease.** Some visitors may not have been inside a Head's study since their own schooldays. Their memories of visits 'to see the Head' from days gone past may have been less than pleasant, so offer the visitors a cup of tea or coffee. If children are present why not offer them a drink, too?

• **Meet during the day** whenever possible. This is not for the convenience of the Head; and very often both parents will have jobs and may find it difficult to come during the day. But day visits provide parents or other visitors with an opportunity to see the school when it is 'at work'. Visitors will then be able to see for themselves what an exciting, lively environment the school provides, with pupils studying purposefully in a disciplined way. A school can be a very 'dead' place when the chlidren have gone home.

• Try to **anticipate the kind of questions** visitors are likely to ask and, more importantly, **have the answers prepared**. Some prospective parents will arrive armed with a list of questions obtained from a newspaper or magazine or from a parents' organisation. Try to read as many examples of such lists as possible, then take a good look at your own school to see how it matches up. You may need to make some changes, or prepare some suitable answers!

THE TOUR

Visitors want to see the school, the children and adults working together. Too many conducted tours give the impression that the school is mainly about the buildings, the classrooms, the hall, the pottery area, etc. Do try to involve pupils and members of staff as much as possible in active, working situations. Include as many 'normal' activities as possible, together with anything particularly interesting which is happening at that time.

The guide

The Head is usually the one to take visitors round the school. In larger schools, however, the task is often assigned to a member of staff and sometimes—very successfully—to senior pupils. A tour of the school with a pupil, followed by a question and answer session with the Head, may be an acceptable mixture of these two styles. The guide, if it is not the Head, must know the way round the school, have read the school prospectus, know something about the school's history and be able to answer questions about the most obvious points on the route. The guide must be eloquent and sensitive to the questions visitors may ask and to the reasons which may lie behind them. The guide should *not* ask the visitors what they want to see, but should have

- planned the route carefully beforehand.

The route
Plan a 'standard' route starting confidently with one of the school's most impressive features – perhaps the assembly hall, library or any building that has recently been opened. It is sometimes a good idea to present a chronological picture starting with the reception area for new pupils and working from there.

Physical education, art or pottery are 'active' lessons which are always interesting to see, but include 'normal' lessons to show how the school values the academic aspects of education, too.

At the beginning of the tour, suggest politely to visitors that you will lead the way, otherwise you will spend the whole of your time grabbing them by the elbow and steering them in the right direction.

Groups
If you are arranging tours for groups of visitors round the school on Open Days, for example, the visit may have to be a shortened one. Try to make sure that the groups are not too large, otherwise those at the back won't be able to hear what is being said, or the guide will have to speak so loudly that they will interrupt any activity which is being watched. It is easy for people to get 'lost' or left behind, so it helps to establish a clear meeting place if this happens. You may need to have a series of departure times if there are lots of groups. Try to arrange things so that the visitors end up at the same time in the school hall for a chance to listen to a short talk by the Head and to raise questions if they wish.

CONCLUSION

Many of the items which have been mentioned in this chapter may seem to be small points in themselves but they all go together to make up 'the hundred little things' which make a big impression on any visitor to the school.

9
The Prospectus and Other Communications

THE SCHOOL PROSPECTUS

A school's prospectus can be regarded as the basis of a contract between the school and parents. It has two important aims:

- To provide parents with essential and useful information about the school;
- To encourage prospective parents to visit the school and to learn more about it.

Essential information
In addition to any LEA regulations, it is suggested that a good prospectus should contain:

- The name and location of the school marked clearly on the front outside cover.
- A brief description of the school's objectives, history and philosophy.
- A good map showing road links.
- Curriculum information.
- Organisation of classes. Average class size and/or pupil teacher ratio.
- Physical description of the school and the teaching areas.
- Facilities for games and sports.
- Artistic and cultural provision including a list of school societies and clubs.
- A brief outline of the school rules and the steps the school may feel bound to take with serious breaches of discipline.
- Arrangements for meals, health and other personal welfare.
- Arrangements for religious worship and instruction and opportunities to be exempt from this.
- List of teaching staff with qualifications.

- Full address of the school and telephone number including one for after school hours.
- Status of the school, eg County or Aided.
- A personal invitation from the Head for the parents to visit the school.

Other useful information which might be included:
- List of Governors.
- Clothing requirements – details of the school uniform.
- School emblems, arms, motto.
- Famous old pupils.

Encouraging parents to visit the school
The information in the prospectus should be set out clearly and without jargon. Photographs and text should convey an impression of a happy school and a family atmosphere. Children must feature prominently. Pictures of empty classrooms will not convey the right atmosphere.

The prospectus may be read by several members of the family including the prospective pupil. Each should find something attractive in the prospectus. The prospectus should not look old fashioned or out-of-date.

Useful points when producing a prospectus

1. Do not be afraid to use **colour** wherever possible. How much colour you use will depend on your budget, but a minimum should be a colourful front cover. This must be eye-catching, preferably with a striking picture of the school. The whole prospectus should not be *too* glossy and extravagant a publication, as parents might question the amount of money spent on this rather than on books or other educational purposes.

2. Choose a **standard paper size** and make sure that it fits 'Post Office preferred envelopes'. A5 is a good size (210 x 148 mm).

3. An advantage in using a **larger printing firm** is that they may have a design and lay-out expert to give you assistance. Also they may be able to keep the print standing so the school can update the prospectus easily. This means the school may not need to have such a large print order initially although enough copies should be printed to last from three to five years.

4. Pages which contain **information which is liable to become out-of-date** quickly should be printed separately and can be included in a pocket at the back of the prospectus. Such information would include: names of staff and present numbers of children on roll.

5. **Pages should be well set out.** Do not cram as many words and photographs on them as you can. White space is an important component in good design; it should be used effectively to make the information easy to absorb. Do not use a hotch-potch of colours and typefaces. One other colour besides black is probably all that is necessary.

6. **Photographs** need not be of uniform size. They should be taken by a professional. If you require a professional photographer and do not know of one, ask the local newspaper.

7. Make sure the prospectus is **accurate** and does not contravene the Trades Descriptions Act!

Where to send your prospectus
Try to ensure that the school's prospectus is seen in as many places as possible in the school's catchment area, but beware of 'overkill' and a reaction against the school. You may well consider sending it, or a condensed version of it, to the places mentioned in Chapter 9 on external communication.

MINI-PROSPECTUS

Some schools print a **condensed version** of their prospectus. They do this either on a single A4 sheet, printed 'sideways' so that the sheet can be folded to make four sides of A5, or (probably with better effect) onto a four page leaflet using the front and back covers of the main prospectus, which are hopefully striking and colourful. The mini-prospectus is designed for the casual as opposed to serious enquirer. You may save some money by distributing the mini-prospectus freely but rationing the full prospectus to serious applicants.

What if the school has only **limited funds** to spend on a prospectus? If colour and glossy paper are to be used, they may only be able to afford a one-sheet prospectus. In this case *something* in colour is better than nothing at all.

Community and busine
enhance primary edu

Objectives

The overriding objective
activities of CLASP is the
enhancement of educat
Sandhurst children in the 5 to 11 yea
group. However, the importance of
community public relations and the
perceived benefits to sponsor compa
also of paramount importance.

Although the standards set at prima
education level directly influence
achievements at secondary and subs
levels, the objectives of CLASP are to
the needs of *primary* education, and
therefore not directly involved with
education at secondary level or above

To achieve its objectives, CLASP is co
to establishing partnerships with co
on a both local and national scale, an
looking towards 1992 and the interr
opportunities that will inevitably aris

Although setting itself high targets f
success, CLASP will never lose sight o
responsibilities to the children in its
the identity, character and ethos of e
its six member schools.

The philosophy of CLASP's approach
full support of Berkshire's Chief Edu
Officer, and provides a major contrib
Berkshire's "Quality in Education" pr

What is CLASP?

There is no question that
primary education lays the
foundation for future learning
and social attitudes. However, this is not
openly recognised by industry and
commerce, and often forgotten by the
community in general.

The increasing freedom for schools to take
on more responsibility for planning and
controlling their own management and
finance structures now provides for new
initiatives in many areas, particularly in that
of community and business partnerships
and liaison.

CLASP is a consortium of six primary schools
in Sandhurst, Berkshire, who are pooling
their resources and managerial talents to
tackle the challenge of putting primary
education in its place as the keystone in our
children's development, and open new doors
in community/education/business links.

CLASP has a formal constitution to ensure
fairness and maximum benefit for the
children in all six member schools,
in its dealings with both commerce
and the community, and its
operations are entirely
independent of the local
education authority.

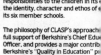

— Community Links Across Sandhurst Primaries —

The CLASP Prospectus

artnerships to on in Sandhurst

The school enviroment can also provide a valuable resource to the business world in terms of work experience and product development opportunity.

If your company or organisation would like to discuss a partnership arrangement, project sponsorship, or supply of equipment or materials, then please contact the headteacher of any of the six CLASP schools.

CLASP recognises the value of PR and is willing to discuss any positive opportunity.

ject Opportunities

There are many on-going work programmes where liaison and partnership possibilities can be ped, including:-

nvironmental issues
ommunications
uilding Works
eacher Placements
chool Visits
usiness Enterprise
lealth and Safety
andscaping
Materials
nformation
echnology

An example of a brochure

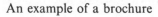

EXAMPLE OF A BROCHURE

An example of a brochure is given on pp 92-93. This is a black and white copy of the inside two pages of a four-page brochure produced by CLASP (Community Links Across Sandhurst Primaries). The original is printed in colour on high quality A3 paper, folded to make four A4 sides, and is laminated. The copy produced here is, therefore, a pale reflection of the original which is striking in its appearance.

The brochure itself sets out clearly the answer to the question 'What is CLASP?' 'CLASP is a consortium of six primary schools in Sandhurst, Berkshire, who are pooling their resources and managerial talents to tackle the challenge of putting primary education in its place as the keystone in our children's development, and open new doors in community/education/business links.'

'The overriding objective in all activities of CLASP is the enhancement of education for Sandhurst children in the 5 to 11 year age group. However, the importance of community public relations and the perceived benefits to sponsor companies are also of paramount importance.'

The brochure is in **full colour**. The background colour of the pages shown is pale blue with the main typescript in black. The headings and the logos are in purple. The information about the schools on the right-hand side has a pink background which tones well with the colour of the logo. This shows how the producers have **not been afraid to use colour**.

A **standard paper size**, A3, has been used.

CLASP used a number of **professional services** to produce this brochure, many of these, but not all, having parental connections with the schools. The ongoing marketing and PR support is provided by Quality Marketing Services, Sandhurst. The brochure design is by B.G. Graphics, Sandhurst, and the brochure printing by Cutlow Ltd, London. This use of professional services to produce a professional product reflects the advice given in this chapter.

The text has been carefully chosen to ensure that the **information does not become out of date**. The headings are 'What is CLASP?', 'Objectives' and 'Project Opportunities' which will not change radically during the life of the partnership. The information about schools does not include the names of Headteachers, for example, which might change.

The **pages are well set out** to make the whole effect one of providing plenty of information which is easy to absorb, but is also attractive to the eye. This requires skill and is another advantage of using professional services.

The photographs, by Simons Studios, Winchester, which include examples of children from each of the schools, are integrated into the whole layout of the brochure. This increases the interest as well as giving further information about the schools involved in the partnership.

The partnership was launched at the Royal Military Academy, Sandhurst and the brochure and the ideas contained in it have been seen in many places within the catchment areas of the schools, as well as reaching a far wider audience.

Quality has its price. This type of brochure is not cheap to produce and CLASP received much sponsorship during the formation of the brochure, not only from the companies mentioned already, but also from British Telecom. CLASP has a continuing dialogue with many local and national companies and organisations but formal partnership/investment arrangements have been established with British Telecom, Rank Xerox, Hewlett Packard, British Airways and Tesco.

The example given here is of a brochure for a group of schools as opposed to the 'usual' single school brochure. This has been done to show how schools can co-operate together, successfully, for educational reasons as well as financial ones. The principles which have been put forward in this chapter should be applied by the reader to their own school brochure to see how it compares. This should then be followed by *action*:the introduction of any changes, major or minor, that need to be made.

OTHER COMMUNICATIONS

Is material from the school informative and visually pleasing? Does it appear as a part of a 'family' with a similar look and 'house style'?

Newsletters

Many schools send out a newsletter, printed on one side of A4, at regular intervals. It is suggested that newsletters should be:

- **High quality**. For all the reasons given previously, *any* publication which is going to all the parents should be of as high a quality as possible. The school might even be advised to invest in some really good quality printing equipment, not only for the printing of newsletters and prospectuses, but also other items indicated later in this chapter.

- **Well set out**. All too often the layout of newsletters is, to say the least, *boring*! Try to make them more interesting by printing 'sideways' and folding to make four sides of A5 instead of one or two sides of A4. The front page should be striking with at least a logo and a *large* headline in a different typeface. The back page can include all the dates for the next month; this means it is easy for the family to put it up somewhere where everybody can see it.

- **Different colour for each month**. The newsletters should be printed on a different coloured paper each month so that they are easily distinguished.

- **Interesting**. There is not only a need for different coloured paper and different print styles, but also readable, varied and informative text. Try to include some humour, items of news about teachers, parents and children and not just notices. How about one or two line illustrations or photographs? (Photographs need better quality paper).

- **Regular**. This means publication at least once a month and every month, not just when you feel like it. The newsletter should always be sent home on the same day of the week and only on that day of the week. All items to be sent home should go on that same day of the week. This means that parents can then ask their children for items on that one day of the week and request another copy of the newsletter if necessary. Needless to say there should be enough printed to allow for this. Keep a record of children who are absent and give them the newsletter when they return.

- Put **'spares' in the local newsagents** where other people might see them.

- Do not send the newsletter just to all parents, but to **everyone else connected with the school** as well. It is being done for publicity and information, after all.

All the above needs *to be managed efficiently and effectively*. This means it needs a person who is in charge of all publicity going out from the school.

School magazines
School magazines are fun and can include worthwhile work in

language. It is worth selling them to the pupils to cover the costs. You may consider sending a magazine with a prospectus to give future pupils and their parents an idea of what the school has to offer. Recent copies of the magazine should be left in the room or place where prospective parents wait before seeing the Head. They should be able to take copies home if they wish to do so.

Videos

Schools are increasingly using video as a marketing tool. A video should be about ten to twenty minutes long. It should be in colour and carefully planned to show the school to its best advantage. Include interesting shots of the school and show the children in both work and leisure activities. The video does not replace the printed prospectus, but it can soon pay for itself by attracting more pupils. Copies may also be sold to current pupils.

A group of schools may get together to make a video, as this way the costs are shared. When commissioning a video it pays to approach two or three companies to get competitive written quotations and to talk about production options. Another way is to contact an expert with a proven record in video-making and ask to view examples of his or her completed work.

OTHER FORMS OF PUBLICATION

If a school has invested in quality printing equipment, as suggested above, it is possible not only to produce high quality printing for the school, but to recoup the initial cost and go on to make money for the school, by printing for others:

- posters for events
- banners and roadside notices
- car stickers
- competitions

THINGS TO SELL

It is possible to print things to sell for the school. These would have the school name and logo on them and could include:

- badges, not only the school badge but badges in general,
- Christmas cards, especially those designed by the children,
- calendars and diaries,

- publications:
  The school magazine
  Where to take your children in the surrounding area
  A Local Celebrity book.

Other things with the school name on it that can be sold for the benefit of the school:

- commemorative souvenirs
- pens and pencils
- photographs not only of individuals, but also of the whole school, teams and classes
- records and tapes
- T-shirts and sweatshirts
- trophies

10
The Media

A comprehensive look at this important area of marketing includes:

- Developing a policy
- What is news?
- Working with the media
- Providing the copy
- Coping with the bad news

DEVELOPING A POLICY

The media are a powerful ally, but can be a dangerous enemy.
When the news is good:

- it gives everybody involved with the school, teachers, parents and children a lift and boosts morale all round;
- it increases identity with the school;
- it creates a sense of pride in the achievements of those mentioned;
- in a wider sense it improves public confidence in the school, and
- helps the school gain a better reputation.

As we saw in previous chapters there is no better method of advertising a school than through word of mouth and to get people talking about the school. It is also worth remembering that good news for one school is good news for all schools, and good for education in general: less harm will be done *when* bad news emerges. Why do so many achievements in school go un-noticed? Why are so many 'good news' stories lost? Surely, everyday good practice in your school can be made just as interesting to the public as extraordinary events and successes.

Good news so often fails to reach the media because the school has neither the inclination nor the time to tell them about it. So who should do this task? It is not yet another job for the Head. It was suggested in Chapter 3 that a team should be set up to manage the marketing of the school. Handling the media is a job which should be done by a member of that team with an aptitude for publicity work, who might even be made 'Press Officer'. Schools need the media to help get their messages out to the community. Each school should decide what is best for them. It should be a conscious decision whether or not to have a press officer and manage the media, and not something into which the school merely drifts.

WHAT IS NEWS?

News is anything which interests a large part of the community and has not been brought to their attention before. News is the product of the media. News is not an event, but the *report* of that event. It is not the actual happening but the story or account of that happening which reaches the public. News is the creation of the newsperson, not the news source. Heads who deal successfully with the media have learned to spot or create events that are newsworthy and to anticipate the reaction of a reporter to a particular happening or situation.

Much of what schools wish to communicate *is* interesting and newsworthy, but it is often not unusual enough to warrant a news item. It's unfortunate, but true, that people doing what they are supposed to do is simply not news. Therefore schools need to remember their other channels of communication, such as news-letters, to publicise that which does not get into the newspapers.

News stories
News stories are immediate, about a particular event, and they convey any information which is interesting or unusual. Events entirely out of the ordinary *are* newsworthy, and no amount of protestation will deter the media. This will be considered in detail later in this chapter; at this stage it is worth saying that the best thing to do in the event of some kind of disaster is to help the reporter obtain accurate information and avoid reporting rumours. The facts are never as damaging as misinformation or misunderstanding.

Features
Features can be an in-depth look at a news story, or a background investigation of a topical issue. Always differentiate between news stories and features. Many a good feature has gone into the News Editor's waste basket and vice versa.

When are schools 'news'?

Regular reading of your local newspapers should give you some idea of the events at your school which might be of interest. Research was carried out on a three-month run of three weekly papers, focused on a small Nottinghamshire town. Every article referring to a local maintained school serving pupils 5 to 18 was identified and studied. From the sample 135 articles were identified: most focused on human interest stories. In more detail, secondary schools were the sole subject of articles on the majority (79) of occasions, primary schools (59) and joint coverage (6) making up the rest. All secondary schools received some mention, compared to only about half of the primary schools. Even after taking into account their smaller size, primary schools seemed much less concerned with, or less adept at, attracting press coverage.

Various newsworthy characteristics of schools have been identified. These include:

- usually very successful in competitive sporting activities;
- visitors frequently enrich the educational diet;
- educational visits are a frequent feature of school life;
- pupils often go into the community to assist and entertain;
- pupils, staff and parent groups are always busy raising money for the school and other 'good causes';
- competitions and quizzes are often entered and won by local schools;
- schools like to spend time celebrating annual events such as Mother's Day, Pancake Day and Easter 'bonnets'.

Schools are therefore the focus of a wide range of activities which do not necessarily represent the day-to-day reality of school life. They do, however, offer a selection of items that meet the criteria for publication of both the school and the newspaper.

Work has been reported on marketing a particular school. This indicated that the school's policy had developed over a number of years and produced two central ideas, the 'frequency strategy' and the 'safety/danger spectrum'.

The **frequency strategy** aimed at this news exposure:

Frequency	Medium	Audience
Weekly	Local newspaper	Local
Monthly	Local radio	Local/regional
Termly	Television	Regional/national

A conscious decision had been made to market the school. In order to achieve the frequencies shown in the table, the monthly school newspaper and the school/industry liaison work in the school was used. The help of a parent who was Director of Marketing for an international company was enlisted and they capitalised on the appointment of a new editor on the local evening newspaper.

The school was shown as being not only a place where institutionalised learning and teaching went on, but also a place for fun and where young people cared about others and the world they inhabited.

The **safety/danger spectrum** idea is that news stories may be located along a continuum depending on their content: this must be borne in mind when approaching the media.

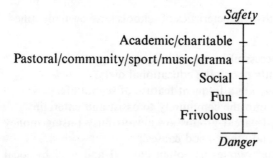

WORKING WITH THE MEDIA

Basic guidelines

- **Be timely** Understand the media's deadlines. Nothing angers a reporter more than a news source who returns a call after the deadline. A shrewd Head understands the deadlines of reporters and instructs other staff members and secretaries what to do about messages. Respecting deadlines is one of the easier ways to build goodwill between school and the media.

- **Be flexible** By its very nature, news is relative. A big story one day may not find space in the paper the next. That means a reporter will not always wait until you are ready to 'release' a story. In some cases you have to be ready to answer the questions when asked.

- **Avoid jargon** 'Criterion-referencing testing' means little if anything to a reporter. Speak plain English. Leave no room for misunderstanding about what you are saying. If you have to use educational terms then be sure to explain them.

- **Don't be defensive** Help the reporter with the story but don't suggest how it should be written. Never ask to see a story before it is run. Respect the reporter's job, but don't stand in awe of him or her.

- **Be honest and open** An educator who appears to be hiding something is only asking for further investigation. School policy should include a procedure for dealing with press enquiries, including who speaks for the school when the Head is not available. The policy should reflect the school's intent to be open and honest. Never say 'no comment' or refuse to answer a legitimate question. A good reporter will keep digging and find the answer elsewhere – and it may *not* be in the form the school would like to see!

- **Avoid speaking off the record** Nothing is every really 'off the record' because reporters can usually obtain information from other sources. It should not be used as a weapon to prevent a reporter from using something which he or she has already learned; the reporter is under *no* legal or ethical obligation to honour it. This is a phrase which is popular with people who are inexperienced at dealing with the press.

- **'For background information only'** may be a better phrase. It means 'Do not quote me as saying what I am going to tell you, but you may use the information as background knowledge in anything you write'. A journalist will protect his sources of information, but is free to find someone else who may be prepared to confirm your statement in direct quotes.

- **'Can we talk around the subject?'** This is a phrase which allows you *time to think*. Try to find out how much the journalist really knows about the situation, and what kind of comment s/he expects you to make. Perhaps only a short crisp comment is wanted. Giving a string of quotes at random is not a viable alternative and does not always produce such a satisfactory result. Another way to give yourself time to think about it is by asking if you can phone the journalist back, but don't forget to do so.

- **Be available** The media really appreciates a news source who is available when needed, and an appreciated news source usually gets 'good press' instead of carping and criticism. But this means being available during non-working hours or even when the story is one which the Head would rather not see in print. Conceding that there are problems and facing them squarely helps a Head's credibility not only with the media, but with the public.

THE ADVANTAGES OF PERSONAL CONTACTS

It is worth the effort, and especially helpful should difficulties arise, to make **personal links** when using the media to promote your school. The following are worth contacting:

Newspapers
Local and 'free' newspapers often welcome regular news items and picture stories from your school. It may help to make your personal links with the 'education correspondent', and if none exists, 'adopt' a journalist. Some schools manage to produce a regular press release; some hints on how to do this are included later.

Radio
Local radio stations remain the most underestimated part of the media by the educational world. A number of the BBC and independent radio stations now have education specialists. Once more make a personal link at the station and send your press release to that person. 'Phone-ins' provide excellent platforms for the school.

    Teachers Weekly recently reported on a school which spent £400 on a local radio advert; it generated much media interest as it was the first school to sell itself to parents on the radio. The 30-second advert was broadcast 15 times a day on Hereward Radio and was professionally produced to publicise the school open evening.

Television
Education makes excellent visual copy and there may be occasional opportunities to promote your school through this medium. A good TV report is worth putting on video and using to show prospective parents, as an alternative to producing your own video.

Radio and TV interviews
From time to time you may be invited to be interviewed by the broadcasting media. You will need to be clear and concise. A useful

tip is to decide the three main points you wish to put across during the interview. You will have done well if you have voiced two of them!

PROVIDING THE COPY

The most efficient way to inform the media and help journalists to get their facts right is through a **press release**. Find out when the deadlines are for your local papers and radio stations; allow journalists as much time as possible to edit your story. Many stories are repeated in a number of newspapers using the same wording, if a press release is circulated. Thus, by 'manufacturing' news, school and not the press can act as definers of newsworthiness.

Sending a story in

Make notes, then compose the story or press release, taking note of all the points which have been made previously in this chapter. Remember the journalist's six questions of Who? What? When? Where? Why? How? Put all the essential information in the first paragraph. Make each paragraph on a further piece of the story complete in itself.

The secret is to **make it easy for the journalist**. Go to your local newspaper and ask them *exactly* how they like the information and then do it in the format that they prefer.

This is the type of thing they might suggest:

- type the story, double or triple spaced
- large margins left and right
- one side of the paper only
- use A4 paper
- keep the press release to one sheet of A4. If you run to more write 'more follows' at the bottom and 'ends' at the end
- get names and facts right
- include names and phone numbers of contacts in school.

When you have done this:

- keep a copy for yourself by the phone
- get somebody else to check the piece
- hand it in personally
- make everything as personal as possible.

Photographs

If you are sending in photographs, remember:

- black and white only
- 8" x 6" minimum print
- sharp contrast
- never use a paper clip to attach things to a photo – it may make it unusable
- do not write on the back of photos; attach a removable sticky label to the back
- send a choice of photos
- always keep copies
- why not write your own caption?

Another way to organise press coverage is to arrange a **photocall** – a time when photographers can visit the school to record a particular event. It may be that you can get the photograph taken separately to go with a press release. It may be possible to phone it in if it is needed quickly.

Getting a reporter out

If you a trying to get a reporter to come to you, you will need to make sure that you 'get in the diary' and that you can answer the question 'What is the appeal of the story?'

Make notes for when the reporter arrives so that you will have all the details to hand.

COPING WITH THE BAD NEWS

- **Don't over-react**

Even the most careful of schools can find itself attacked in the media. Angry phone calls or a nasty letter to the editor may fuel the flames. A reasoned response to an inaccurate story or unfair criticism usually gets some space or air-time, but it's unreasonable to demand equal space or equal time. In the final analysis, is it really worth destroying a good working relationship? At the time it might seem devastating, but what will be the long term impact of bad news? How many people really saw it? How many really *care*? How many people will *really* let it change their attitudes about the school? The chances are good that the incident will be forgotten quickly.

Do not see the media as adversaries because, 'Never argue with anyone who buys ink by the barrel and paper by the ton'. Recognise the reality that in a head to head battle between the school and the media, the media have the advantage.

There are a few **key principles** which you should know about and be able to apply in order to communicate effectively under pressure. The time to learn these is before the crisis occurs and the time to practise them is when there is no panic. It's too late for preparation after the emergency strikes.

Anticipation and **preparation** are cornerstones to good communication. It is essential to have the facts, decision and policies clearly in your mind before you meet your audience. Look for early warning signs, for example if the numbers on roll have fallen dramatically or if the results of the stage 1 assessment are not as good as you would have liked.

In planning to tell your story be guided by three principles:

- truth
- completeness
- position

Truth
Be *prepared* to tell the truth, even if it seems painful at the time. Give an honest answer. The truth is more *practical*. You cannot cover up the truth anyway. The truth is more *effective*. You want to raise trust in you and your school, so don't be caught in deception. Trust and confidence grow if you're honest with your answers.

Completeness
Tell the *whole* truth. Hiding information damages your credibility.

Position
Position your answers. Tell your audience *why* you have taken the action you have, and continue with the reasons so that these are connected.

CHECKLIST: DEALING WITH A CRISIS

Prepare a statement about the incident
Make it brief and factual. It must be correct and not misleading. It should include information which reflects positively on the school and which is relevant.

Referred telephone calls
Arrange for all telephone calls to be referred through a competent secretary to the one person who should handle all enquiries. Usually this person should be the Head, but sometimes it is better handled by the Chairman of the Governors or deputy. The secretary should take the name of the caller, and of the organisation, and telephone number. The secretary can also read over the statement and act as a buffer if the school has nothing else to add.

Home calls
Reporters are skilled at discovering home telephone numbers and addresses quickly, so arrange for someone else to answer the telephone and the door.

Playing for time
If a reporter rings before you have a statement prepared – play for time. Say that you will look into the matter and ring the reporter back. Do not be hustled into making a statement. Resist the temptations:

- to ask how the reporter found out about the incident – you will not be told and you have confirmed that it has happened;
- to give an off-the-cuff comment or to discuss the incident generally.

When reporters arrive
If a reporter visits, get him or her shown into a waiting room. Be polite. Reporters will respond to being treated civilly. On the other hand, they should not be allowed to wander about the school asking questions of pupils and staff.

Talking to reporters
Stick to the statement. Do not say more than you have to, but deny facts that are put to you which are wrong. Make it clear that the only direct quotation that you want to appear in the paper is the prepared statement. Keep a careful record of what is said. If you have had a rather long and muddled conversation, ask the journalist to read over what you are going to be quoted as saying.

Instructions to staff
Staff should be informed at an early stage of the steps that are being

taken. They should be asked to refer all enquiries to the Head or person in charge of answering them.

Instructions to pupils
It is advisable to tell pupils not to talk to journalists or to anyone else outside the school about the incident. They should also be warned not to be persuaded by photographers to pose for photographs.

Parents
Write a letter to parents of children at the school after the incident has been given wide and harmful publicity, to reassure them and include your statement to the press.

Photographs
A photograph can often do more damage than the printed word. Photographers cannot be prevented from taking photographs unless they trespass on school property.

A FINAL COMMENT

Be assured that most news in the newspapers is positive. Although using the media requires some hard thinking, attention to detail and also enthusiasm, the rewards which are to be had in motivation and public relations are sure to make it all worthwhile.

PRESS RELEASES

Two examples of possible press releases are given below, together with further comments.

CREWEALSA PRIMARY SCHOOL
ALSA ROAD, CREWEALSA, CA1 1AC

Contact: Headteacher Brian Hardie   0270 252500 (school)
                                                              0270 525522 (home)

PRESS INFORMATION FOR IMMEDIATE RELEASE 5th June

HEADTEACHER RUNS MARATHON

The Headteacher of Crewealsa Primary School, Brian Hardie, aged 45, completed the London Marathon in three hours and six minutes on Sunday 4th June 1990 to raise sponsorship money to buy a computer for the school.

Mr Hardie has been in training for the event for over a year and has increased his running each week up to a maximum of eighty-seven miles in one week. This is an average of over twelve miles for each day of the week. Two weeks before the marathon he started to 'taper' for the big event by doing mainly short runs.

'I have been training hard as I did not want to disappoint the children, the parents and all those involved with Crewealsa Primary School,' he said before the event.

Mr Hardie was sponsored by parents, governors and local industry in order to buy a new Archimedes computer for the children's use in the school. Mr Hardie said, 'We need the most up-to-date technology for today's children who are the citizens of tomorrow.'

Sufficient money was raised to purchase the computer and also a trolley on which to put it. The equipment will be presented to the school at a special assembly in the school hall on Monday 11th June at 9.30 a.m. to which all parents, governors and sponsors from local industry who supported Mr Hardie in his venture are invited.

ENDS

CREWEALSA PRIMARY SCHOOL
ALSA ROAD, CREWEALSA, CA1 1AC

Contact: Headteacher Brian Hardie   0270 252500 (school)
                                                              0270 525522 (home)

PRESS INFORMATION FOR IMMEDIATE RELEASE 3rd September

PARENTS AND TEACHERS WORK TOGETHER
TO PREPARE SCHOOL FOR NEW TERM

Parents and teachers have worked together to prepare the school for the first day of term on Monday 3rd September after Crewealsa Primary School was broken into at some time during the night of Saturday 1st September. A number of items were stolen. There was more mess than damage.

Crewealsa Primary School was broken into some time during the night of Saturday 1st September. The following items were stolen: a 26" colour television, a video recorder, £8.34 in cash from the 'petty cash' tin and a number of pencils and felt-tip pens. Damage was caused to the cupboard door where the television and video were stored. The secretary's desk where the cash was locked away and the filing cabinets in the secretary's room were also damaged. A small fire had been started in the Headteacher's study in the wastepaper bin, but this did not spread. The vandals had taken all the papers out of the filing cabinets and thrown them round the Head's study and in the adjacent corridor. A trail of destruction followed in every one of the classrooms. Desks and chairs were overturned, books had been taken from the piles prepared for the beginning of term and thrown about the rooms. Paint was daubed on the books, walls and floor. In the Library all the books had been pulled off the shelves and scattered on the floor.

Twenty parents, all nine staff of the school including the Head, Mr Brian Hardie and the Caretaker, Fred James, worked all day Sunday to clear up the mess that had been caused. Although Mrs Valerie Beattie's first year junior classroom will need some redecoration the school was ready for opening on the first day of term.

'It was a great piece of teamwork to get everything ready for the children at the beginning of a new school year,' said Brian Hardie, the Headteacher.

ENDS

Comments

- The **name and address of the school** are given, and headed notepaper may be used for this purpose.
- The **name** and home and office **telephone numbers** are given of a contact in case any further information is required. Journalists do not necessarily work school hours, hence the need for a home contact number. You may decide that you do not wish to give this number.
- **Press information** helps to identify the document and direct it within the newspaper office.
- The **release date** allows you to send in immediate information or in advance.
- The **date** is essential for record purposes.
- The **headline** is short, simple and to the point.
- **The first paragraph gives all the essential information.**
- The **Who? What? Where? When? Why? and How?** are considered in the next paragraph.
- **Direct quotations** are included wherever possible.

11
Marketing Evaluation

This is the final part of the marketing cycle—or is it the first? As mentioned earlier the seeking for information may be seen as a part of quality control, whereas the answers may be marketing research. Either way, this section is an important part of the marketing cycle and should not be omitted under any circumstances. Evaluation should not be seen as threatening; rather it is an opportunity to see what can be improved or put right in the school. It should be seen as a chance to establish an approach which is appropriate to education in the 1990s, central to which is the idea of 'client satisfaction'.

There are two reasons why we need a monitoring and evaluation programme:

- to find out whether the clients *are* satisfied
- to compare the implementation of the marketing plan with what actually resulted.

This evaluation again needs to be:

- comprehensive
- systematic
- objective
- periodic

and will involve:

- the collection of information
- the analysis of the information

This similarity to the Marketing Audit is not accidental: it allows for evaluation to be used as the beginning of a second cycle when appropriate.

As before the information may be collected by:

- questionnaires in newsletters
- spot telephone surveys
- meetings with key communicators

and the information used, perhaps, to produce a **database** which could be used for reference in the future.

QUALITY MONITORING

Quality monitoring allows schools to review their academic and other services *taking a client-centred perspective*. After collection of information the first analysis will produce some indicators of performance. However, performance indicators do simply *indicate*. They are crude measures and offer an insubstantial basis for detailed decision making. However, by providing an overview they create the opportunity for better targeting of the limited resource available for the investigation of areas which, by client testimony, show up as particular problems or successes.

Performance indicators may be set by others, such as the LEA or Central Government, especially the National Curriculum test results; they will all assume a greater importance in the future, to the clients, both parents and pupils, of all schools. If these indicators are not to overwhelm all other indicators of school performance, then it is up to all of us in education to educate the parents yet again. Nevertheless these performance indicators of one kind or another *will* be used. Perhaps the answer is to write our own.

Writing performance indicators

There are two types of performance indicator, those for carrying out tasks, and those designed for objective setting. Performance indicators should consist of a single sentence for both of these types. In each sentence there should be, in this order, a verb, a direct object of the action and a result.

For example: Develop guidelines to introduce the National Curriculum.

Verb	Develop...
Direct object or action	...guidelines...
Result	...to introduce the National Curriculum

- in other words performance indicators should start with a verb, specify only 'what' and avoid 'how'.

- Examples of verbs for carrying out of the task might be: achieve, assess, evaluate, identify, improve, maintain, specify and supervise.

- and for objective setting: approve, define, develop and prepare.

- They should once again be SMART, Specific, Measurable, Attainable, Realistic and may also be Time constrained.

Examples for the carrying out of tasks
Achieve... the writing of science guidelines... by the end of term.
Assess... the number of children... with special educational needs.
Evaluate... community involvement... in the life of the school.
Identify... parental involvement... in the classroom.
Improve... pupil attitudes... towards co-operative play.
Maintain... good relationships... between governors and staff.
Specify... the number of courses... attended by teachers in a year.
Supervise... the level of oil in the tank... at the time of delivery.

Examples of objective setting
Approve... safety measures... to reduce the rate of accidents in the playground.
Define... the number of staff... needed for playground duty.
Develop... lesson plans... for science teaching.
Prepare... plans... for the introduction of technology.

More detailed information
As suggested earlier, indicators show up a particular success or possible problem. This indication needs to be followed up with a series of one-to-one interviews with clients to obtain more detailed information. A report then needs to be prepared, summarising and analysing the points made in the interviews. This report may help in the evaluation of the problem. It may help to identify whether it is viewed as an issue connected with:

- communication
- resources
- staff development or
- the marketing process itself

Having completed this evaluation we need to ask the question: how does the school match up in the eyes of the clients? Are the clients showing how they feel about the performance of the school with their feet? Take a good look at numbers on roll, and any apparent trends over the past three or four years.

This takes us back to the question: what are we going to do about it?

What action are we going to take? We shall have to try to take action to improve the school, but the very fact that we are *trying* to do something means that the clients are likely to be less dissatisfied.

It must be emphasised again that marketing is *not* about 'selling' and 'conning' people into believing that which is untrue. Marketing is about producing a high quality education for all children which is then communicated to as wide an audience as possible.

Activities

Some of the questions which have been asked in this chapter are now presented in a form which may make them easier to use as activities.

PERFORMANCE INDICATORS

What are the **performance indicators** which are of interest to your clients?

Indicator   *Client groups interested*

How do you match up to these Performance Indicators?

Indicator   *How well matched*

In order to **find out** you could:
- send questionnaires in newsletters
- do spot telephone surveys, or
- meet with key communicators, for example:
  Parents   *Ex-parents*   *Ex-pupils*

What questions might you ask?

1.

2.

3.

Take a good look at the numbers on roll and any trends there may have been over the past three or four years.

YOUR COMPETITIVE EDGE

Dennison in *Competitive Edge: Attracting More Pupils* suggests there are 25 factors which represent a school's 'competitive edge'. How do you match up to this list?

1. **Quality of the buildings**
   Do the buildings appear attractive, clean and looked after?
   Do we display special features to best effect – playing fields, pottery area?

2. **Location**
   How many children live within reasonable travelling distance?
   How easy is it to travel to this school rather than others? Crossing of main roads?

3. **History of the school**
   Is there a tradition in the local community of attending the school?
   Do we publicise the best features of the school's recent history?

4. **Nature of the catchment area**
   Do we have a 'natural' catchment area?
   Why might children in this area want to attend other schools?

5. **The 'caring' school**
   Are we seen as a 'caring' school – towards parents and pupils?
   Are relationships between pupils, teachers and parents thought to be good?

6. **Organisation of parents' evening and other visits to schools**
   Are parents' evenings well organised?
   Are teachers well prepared and able to answer questions?

7. **Examination results**
   What do outsiders think of our examination results?
   What are our test scores at 7 and 11 likely to be, relative to other schools?

8. **Quality of teaching?**
   How is the quality and quantity of our teaching perceived –
   homework policy?
   Are particular styles and attitudes thought to dominate?

9. **Extra-curricular activities**
   Have we extra-curricular activiites which attract pupils – music,
   sport etc?

10. **HMI/LEA reports**
    Can we use a 'good' report to illuminate what we do well?
    What can we do to avoid an adverse report and related publicity?

11. **Length and arrangement of the school day?**
    Do parents find the organisation of the school day attractive?
    Are we sufficiently aware of our custodial responsibilities?

12. **Children's behaviour outside school**
    How do children seem to behave entering and leaving the
    premises?
    Are there complaints from the public about the children's
    behaviour outside the school?

13. **Children's behaviour inside school**
    What are the parental and public perceptions about children's
    behaviour in lessons?
    Do outsiders think we apply the appropriate 'code of discipline'?

14. **Links with feeder schools and groups**
    How firm are our links with feeder schools, nurseries and
    playgroups?
    Do staff in feeder schools perceive (and purvey to parents and
    children) the firmness of the links?

15. **Links with receiving schools and FE, HE, employers**
    If the attractiveness of a recipient institution declines will it affect
    our recruitment?

16. **School uniform**
    Is there a policy on school uniform?
    How effectively do outsiders think this policy is pursued?

17. Unofficial grapevine
What does the unofficial grapevine think (and say) about the school – in shops, offices, pubs and homes?

18. Quality of information sent to parents
Do we send good quality information to parents?
How do we check the time and condition in which it arrives home?

19. Quality of the brochure
Is our brochure of good enough quality?
Does it demonstrate the full range of pupil opportunities?

20. Number of feeder schools receiving brochure
How many potential feeder schools and other organisations receive our brochure?

21. Adverse comments on competitor schools
Can we (ought we) to use comments made about neighbouring schools by parents, HMI, LEA officers?

22. Media comments
Does the local press imply that we are a good school?
If not can we change the situation?

23. Volume of good publicity
Is every opportunity taken to ensure good publicity about pupil achievement, team successes, etc?

24. Community involvement
To what extent does the local community feel involved in the school?
Can we extend any commitment to include a larger group of people?

25. Profile of the Head, staff, governors
How well known are the Head, staff and governors in the local community?
Do people seem to want to be associated with the school?

Are there any other factors which you think are significant to *your* school?

ARE THE CLIENTS SATISIFIED?

This checklist was devised by four Headteachers, Sister Aquinas, Tony Arrowsmith, Jim Curley and Sheila Stringer who suggest that: 'Parents appreciate high standards achieved by a balanced curriculum in a disciplined working atmosphere which is warm and friendly. They appreciate staff who are caring and accessible.'

How can our marketing indicate that we are meeting these expectations?

Internal factors

School buildings and environs

Position_____

Attractiveness_____

Uniqueness_____

Cleanliness_____

Maintenance_____

Car Parking_____

Name of school clearly shown_____

Entrance hall_____

Rooms adjacent to the hall_____

Interior/exterior decoration_____

Cloakrooms_____

Floor surfaces_____

Display boards_____

Historical aspect of building_____

Space_____

Headteacher

Personality – friendliness, approachability, warmth_____

Appropriate dress_____

Confident_____

Time given_____

Pride and dedication_____

Staff and children

Friendliness_____

Warmth of reception_____

Relationships with one another_____

Relationships with Head and other adults_____

Size of the classes_____

Curriculum

Indications of high standards – work book displays_____

Work practices in appropriate situations_____

Evidence of progression_____

Resources

  library_____

  reading scheme display_____

  maths/science areas_____

  computers_____

  AVA_____

  music, craft/CDT, art, PE, RE_____

Evidence of activities – photographs, videos, trophies,
  gold and silver discs_____

Exhibitions_____

Discipline

Children's movement round the school_____

Uniform_____

Children's attitude to work, to each other and
  to the teachers_____

Noise levels_____

Manners_____

Tidiness_____

Openness_____

Information

Information entrance hall_____

Amount and quality of literature, ie school prospectus_____

Parents' notice board_____

Newsletter_____

Video_____

Photographs_____

Free samples_____

External factors

Taking the school into the Community

Displays in areas used by the public_____

Performances_____

School visits_____

Travel to and fro_____

Press_____

Television_____

Links with other schools, eg sports_____

Contacting new arrivals in the neighbourhood_____

Bringing the community into the school

Parents helping in school_____

PTA_____

Social events_____

School celebrations_____

Fund raising events_____

Sports_____

External use of school resources_____

Visiting professionals and performers_____

Polling day_____

- They suggest that the best way to keep, or increase, pupil numbers is to **open a nursery class**.

DID WE DO WHAT WE PLANNED?

The object of this valuation is to compare the marketing *plan* with what *actually* happened.

Which of the activities we planned, did we complete?

Activity   *How well completed*

Which of the activities we planned, did we *not* complete?

Activity   *Stage reached*

Why did we not complete them?

Lack of effort?

Lack of time?

Lack of resources?

Other reasons?

12
A Case Study

This case study of a real school has been included to assist the reader to see the whole marketing process in action. Details of the names of people or places concerned with the school have been changed, but in all other respects this is an accurate representation of the processes and outcome of the recent introduction of the marketing cycle into one particular school.

Information on the school can currently be obtained from the Northshire Schools Information booklet which is the only written information available to the parents at present. This seven-page typewritten A5 booklet is of a standard format for all schools in the county. It has a pale blue cover and does not include any photographs, diagrams or pictures.

Pennine County Primary School is a co-educational day school administered by the Northshire County Council. It is on the outskirts of a large city in the north west of England. It caters for pupils between five and eleven years of age. The number on roll is 450. The school was built in 1940 and is set in a pre-war council housing estate. About 95% of the children in the school come from this large estate and about 60% of the children are receiving free school meals. Within the 'official' catchment area of the school is a newer 'middle class' area of housing. Most of these children go to the Grampian Church of England Aided Primary School which involves a longer walk. About thirty children from this area do come to Pennine School.

The School buildings are in a similar state of disrepair to many others in the county, and there is considerable exterior dilapidation. The teachers have attempted to make the most of the interior of the school by putting up many colourful displays of the children's work. The school is a large one with many entrances and corridors, and there are notices to help visitors find their way to the Head's room and Secretary's office.

Many of the five-year-old pupils have already attended the Pennine Nursery School, a totally separate school on a site adjacent to the primary school. The primary school admits children into the reception class in September, January and April. The children work in mixed ability classes, but are grouped according to the needs within the class structure.

In the infant department welfare assistants help in the reception classes and the emphasis throughout is on the teaching of reading, writing and numbers. The hope is to have a happy, hard-working school where children feel secure and can develop to the best of their abilities. They are encouraged to speak politely, with clarity and confidence.

There are a large number of children with learning difficulties, who were catered for in the Specific Learning Difficulties Department. Unfortunately, this has had to be disbanded with the current level of staffing. The children are now catered for in their normal classes where their progress is carefully monitored and work is structured to their ability level.

The policy is to give the children as broad an educational experience as possible and the full range of subjects is covered. Sex education is not taught at the school. Religious education is a compulsory part of the curriculum and there is an assembly each day.

A house system operates throughout the school, using colours in the infant department and names of colours in the junior department. There is house competition with awards during each term. House captains and vice-captains are appointed.

There is no rigid policy for homework, but this can be set on request. In certain circumstances a reading book may be taken home and spelling lists and 'tables' will be supplied by the class teachers.

A report is sent to parents annually on their children's progress for which a signature of receipt is required. Three Open Evenings are held each year when parents are invited to come into school to discuss their children's achievements with classteachers. The attendance at these evenings is about 70% over the year.

Discipline in school is considered to be very important, but in accordance with the Education Act 1986, corporal punishment will not be administered in county schools maintained by Northshire County Council Education Committee.

The house system has been adapted to include a punishment system of order marks. If a child is given two, a daily report system will be instituted—a third will mean the involvement of parents. Order marks cover work, attitude and behaviour. Suspension is used and for antisocial behaviour at lunchtimes a child may be sent home for a period of time. This system is gradually replacing corporal punishment which is being phased out.

The school enters teams in a number of competitive sports: soccer, cricket, netball, rounders, swimming and athletics. Other extra-curricular activities include: gymnastics club, sports aerobic club and various team coaching sessions. There are two small school orchestras, a school choir involving sixty children and infant recorder groups.

As will be seen from these details, Pennine County Primary is a traditional urban school, with the staff set in their ways of doing things. One member of the staff, a curriculum co-ordinator, decided, after a course on 'Marketing the Primary School', to follow the procedure recommended in this book.

DEVELOPING A TEAM

At a staff meeting on 5th September the staff were invited to join a marketing team. A small team of four volunteers came together following this staff meeting. This team has since increased to six following the 'report back' session to staff. This team consists entirely of members of staff and includes the Head and a scale 'C' postholder who is a member of the senior management team of the school.

The following week on 12th September this team had its first meeting. They conducted a SWOT analysis of the school with the following results.

SWOT analysis

Strengths

Well-established school.

• Music	Well known for school productions, although little money has been spent on these in the past.
• Friendly atmosphere	In spite of the area in which the school is situated, the atmosphere of the school is a friendly one.
• Nursery school	There is a nursery school next door to the school. Although this is a separate school it does attract pupils. Unfortunately not all of these subsequently move on to Pennine Primary; many go to Grampian.

- High School   The local secondary school is well thought of.
- Elderly residents   Good relationships with nearby old people's
                       home.

Weaknesses
The following areas were seen to be 'poor' and in urgent need of
improvement
  - Reputation and image of the school.
  - Parent/school relationships.
  - Standard of behaviour by children outside the school.
  - Not attracting all the children in the catchment area, particularly
    those 'quality children' from the 'middle class' homes.

Opportunities
This section also included some 'remedies' to the perceived
weaknesses.
  - Private building in the area is continuing.
  - Use of local radio, which is strong in the area.
  - School productions are always 'sold out', so:
      increase the number of performances;
      invite sponsorship or local advertising;
      perform in a more central theatre to a wider audience.
  - Increase contact with nearby old people's home by:
      giving 'special' performances for them;
      keeping them informed of the day-to-day life of the school.
  - P.T.A.—forming an 'official' Parent Teacher Association. The
    timing of this is important as it needs to be set up before
    fostering other links.
  - Increased parental involvement in the school.
  - Improved written communication with parents—production of a
    news-sheet.
  - Improved internal discipline leading to improved external
    discipline.

Threats
The numbers of children in the catchment area who are going to
other schools:
  - Grampian Church-Aided Primary School's numbers of roll are
    increasing.
  - Catholic primary school in the area provides transport for its
    pupils.

Aims and objectives
The team also produced some long-term and short-term objectives.

Long-term aims
- Improve the exterior of the building.
- Increase parental involvement in the school.

Short-term objectives
- Produce a school uniform policy.
- Form an 'official' Parent Teacher Association.
- Improve written communication with parents by producing a news-sheet by the end of term.

These short-term objectives can now be taken in turn to record the progress with each of them.

School uniform
The Head has sent a letter to the parents at the end of July encouraging the wearing of school uniform by the children at the beginning of the new school year. At the beginning of term about 25% of the children were in uniform.

At the Staff Meeting on 18th September the following decisions were made:

- To have a school uniform policy, namely the 'encouraging' of the wearing of school uniform by the children. This was to be carried out by class teachers in their own classes. Not all the teachers were in favour of the policy, because, 'You'll never get the children in this area to wear uniform.'
- To set up a uniform shop after school to be run by one of the teachers:
    to sell school ties and badges which are already available, but worn by very few children;
    to have a second-hand section for clothes which children have grown out of but not worn out.
- To provide new kit for the sports teams as soon as funds become available.

Links were set up with local shops to ensure they had supplies of the relevant clothes.
Parents agreed to help with the uniform shop.
2nd October—Uniform shop sold out of ties!

5th October—Evaluation of uniform policy at a marketing team
meeting showed that an amazing 86% of the children
in the school were now in uniform. This result was
calculated by a group of children as a part of their
maths lesson and involved using computers.

Parent Teacher Association
At the Staff Meeting on 18th September the following decision were
made:

- To invite the parents to form a PTA.
- To have more parental involvement in the school.

On 27th September, following the Annual Meeting of Governors
with Parents, those twenty-seven parents and teachers who were in
attendance had their first meeting of the PTA and decided to form an
'official' Parent, Teachers and Friends Association with the election
of a Chairperson, Vice-chair, Secretary, Treasurer and Assistant
Treasurer.

On 17th October at the second meeting of the PTAFA there were
thirty-five members present and they made the following decisions:

- To develop the relationships between parents and staff.
- To have some fund-raising events, the following being planned:
  A 'baking day' on Monday 5th November when parents would
  come into school to make and sell items they have baked with
  the children and elsewhere. A letter, written by one of the
  parent members of the committee, was sent home.
  A junior disco on Friday 7th December.
  A puppet show in December on a date to be finalised.
- To have some social events:
  A 60s disco was planned for next term.
- Long term—a fête was planned for the summer term.

The News Sheet
This is now well in hand and the first news-sheet is planned for the
beginning of December.

MARKETING DIARY

These events are now presented in the form of a diary to show the
chronology of the *whole* process so far.

Date	Activity	Outcome
September 5th	Staff meeting	Staff invited to join marketing team
September 12th	First marketing meeting	Long-term aims Short-term objectives School uniform policy Need for PTA Improve written communications

September 18th	Staff meeting	Decisions on:
		  Uniform policy
		  Set up uniform shop
		  Invite parents to form PTA
		  More parental involvement
		  New kit for sports teams

September 27th	Annual Governors' meeting 1st PTAFA meeting	Parents who attended set up new PTAFA
October 2nd	Uniform shop	Parent helpers in shop Sold out of ties!
October 5th	Marketing meeting	Uniform evaluation 86% clad Improve look of building New reception area News-sheet action planning
October 8th	Parent helpers	In the Infant school

October 17th	2nd PTA meeting	Fund-raising acts
		  Baking day
		  Junior disco
		  Puppet show
		Social—60s disco
		Long-term—summer fête

OTHER DEVELOPMENTS

Music—which was seen as a strength in the SWOT analysis.
In order to increase and use this perceived strength it has been decided to put up a 'Music Notice Board' to communicate what is happening in this strong area of the school to both pupils and parents.

It has been arranged for the choir to go to the old people's home to sing carols towards the end of term when it is near Christmas.

A 'Grandparents' afternoon' has been planned for later in the term. It has been shown that grandparents have a great influence on the reputation of a school as they pass on so much by word of mouth.

Discipline—which was seen as a weakness outside the school.
There has been a concerted effort by the staff to improve the discipline *internally* in the school, in the playground, the corridors

and the dining hall, before the more difficult area of discipline and behaviour *externally* to the school is tackled.

Curriculum resourcing

Curriculum resourcing has always in the past been undertaken centrally, by the Headteacher. Within the general climate of greater communication and involvement by the staff, the resourcing responsibilities of the subject co-ordinators have been increased. This has resulted in an increased interest by the staff in their subject areas and, hopefully, this will be reflected in the interest which is shown by the children. This in turn may increase the academic achievements of the children resulting in another marketing opportunity.

COMMENTS ON THE WHOLE MARKETING PROCESS AT PENNINE PRIMARY SCHOOL

The school which has been chosen for this case study was an 'opportunity sample' by the author and his contact with one teacher. This teacher showed, however, what can be achieved by the initial enthusiasm of one person, which is passed on to a team and then to a wider audience both inside and outside of one school.

The second point is that great strides have been made in the very short time of half a term. It may be that this rapid progress cannot be maintained, but it is surprising what happens once the 'snowball' starts to roll. Nothing breeds success like success. In this success story more teachers and parents are being involved because marketing and reputation management have been seen to be successful in the school.

It might be that in this particular school where there was no formal association of parents and teachers, where parents had not been involved in the past, where uniform existed but had fallen into disuse, that it would be easy to generate enthusiasm for the school. There was, however, considerable apathy, disinterest and past failure to overcome. Comments such as:

'You'll never get the parents of the school interested.'

'You'll never get the children in this school to wear uniform.'

'You'll never get the parents in this school to come to a disco.'

are not uncommon elsewhere.

If there can be progress at Pennine County Primary School in a 'difficult' urban area, surely there can be progress in your school, wherever it is in the country.

Glossary

DEN (Distinctive Educational Niche). A technique to assist with the development of the unique qualities of the school.

GRIST (Grant Related In-Service Training). A former method by which the Government funded the in-service training of teachers.

LEA (Local Education Authority). The organisation which manages schools within a county or metropolitan borough.

LEATGS (Local Education Authority Training Grants Scheme). The method by which the Government now funds the in-service training of teachers.

LMS (Local Management of Schools). A scheme by which schools have control over their own budgets.

PAC (Performance, Actual Conditions, Capabilities). A technique for the systematic analysis of the school for market research.

SDP (School Development Plan) A plan for the whole school which has been a requirement of the 1988 Education Act.

SWOT (Strengths, Weaknesses, Opportunities, Threats). A technique for the systematic analysis of the school for market research.

USP (Unique Selling Point). A special quality that is unique to one particular school.

Further Reading

There are no books—apart from this one—on the marketing of the primary school, at the present time. There are, however, some books on the marketing of *other* types of schools and organisations, which are recommended. The first publication on the list is particularly useful.

Public Relations
Bland, Michael, *Be Your Own PR Man* (Kogan Page)

Independent schools
ISIS, *Good Communications Guide* (Independent Schools Information Service, 1986)

American schools
AASA, *Skills for Successful School Leaders* (American Association of School Administrators, 1985)

Educational Institutions
Kotler, P & Fox, *Strategic Marketing for Educational Institutions* (Prentice-Hall, 1985)

Industry
McBurnie, T & Clutterbuck, D, *The Marketing Edge* (Penguin, 1988)

Useful articles
There are also a number of articles which have been referred to in the text of this book which the reader would benefit from reading in the original.

CSCS, 1986, *Broadsheet 12: Schools and the Media*; *Broadsheet 17: Schools in the Market-place* (Centre for the Study of Comprehensive Schools).

Dennison, W, 1989(a), 'The Competitive Edge – attracting more pupils', *School Organisation*, Vol 9 No 2.

Evonic, I, 1988, 'Communicating Under Pressure', *Drake Business Review*, Vol 3 No 1.

Gorman, G, 1988, 'Get on the media map' in *Teacher's Weekly*, 24.10.88.

Hart, D, 1990, 'Parent power, school problems', *The Times*, 15.1.90.

Hughes, M, Wikeley, F, & Nash, P, 1990, 'Business partners' *Times Educational Supplement*, 5.1.90.

Reeves, G & Capel, M, 1989, 'Presenting a Primary School Image' *Management in Education*, Vol 3 No 3.

Tilling, M & Walker, K, 1988, 'Marketing at Pindar School' in *Management in Education*, Vol 2, No 1, Spring 1988.

Williamson, P, 1989, 'What the papers say' in *The Times Educational Supplement* 3.2.89.

Index

More books on Education Management

The following pages contain details of a selection of other titles on Education Management. For further information, and details of our Inspection Copy Service, please apply to:

Northcote House Publishers Ltd, Plymbridge House, Estover Road, Plymouth PL6 7PZ, United Kingdom. Tel: Plymouth (0752) 705251. Fax: (0752) 777603. Telex: 45635.

A selection of catalogues and brochures is usually available on request.

Local Management of Schools
Brent Davies & Chris Braund

Written by two consultants in this important field, this book meets the pressing need for an introductory handbook to help governors, teachers and parents get to grips with major new responsibilities now becoming mandatory. Readable and practical, the book spells out the new legislation and what it means, the new financial structure in secondary and primary schools, the new role of Head teachers and governors in delegated school management, and what it means for the future. Complete with case studies and suggested management exercises.

'The nine main chapters, each dealing with a different aspect, are easy to read, comparatively jargon-free, and gave me a very good overview of LMS.... This reference book will justify a place in any educational establishment because of its accessible information and advice.' *Junior Education*. 'Well favoured by the brevity/practicality formula, written with governors and parents in mind as well as teachers. It is strong on illustrative yet simple graphics and tables and does not shirk the consequences of falling numbers.' *Times Educational Supplement*

Paperback, 96 pages, tables.

The School Development Plan
From Draft to Action
Chris Braund

The Education Reform Act 1988 will soon require each of the 28,000 state primary and secondary schools in Britain to draw up and put into action their own School Development Plan. In this document they must define the human, financial and physical resources available to them, and show how these resources will be used to attain specified goals within a specified timescale. Written by a specialist at the forefront of education management *School Development Plans* will be welcomed as an urgently needed step-by-step manual to help every head teacher and governor understand and master this new procedure which will be so important for the future success of their school in today's deregulated environment.

Contents: Introduction, drawing up the school's mission statement, how to carry out the school audit, planning for the school's development, turning plans into action, taking stock and reporting progress, overview, case study, suggested management exercises, glossary, further reading, index.

A Cambridge graduate, Chris Braund MA PGCE MPhil MEd is a Senior Lecturer in Education Management at Crewe & Alsager College of Higher Education, and Programme Leader for its fulltime MSc course in Education Management. He is actively concerned with training school heads from all over Britain in school management skills, and is a former Regional Committee Member of the British Education Management Association.

Paperback, approx 128 pages, illustrated.

Managing the Primary School Budget
Brent Davies & Linda Ellison

With the framework of the Local Management of Schools firmly in place, heads, staff and governors need to turn their attention to its implementation at the local school level.

This practical guide begins by establishing the key dimensons of LMS and reviews the nature of income and expenditure in the primary school. It moves on to a consideration of the way in which budgeting fits into school management development planning and examines the role of staff and governors in the process.

The book then adopts a step-by-step approach using a case study school to demonstrate how to go through the three key stages of budgetary review, planning and implementation. This will provide primary schools with a practical framework enabling them to manage their new-found financial responsibilities.

Brent Davies BA MSc is Head of Educational Management at Crewe + Alsager College and is an LMS adviser to a large number of local education authorities. He has provided LMS management training for over 1000 primary heads in differing LEAs. He is the author of *Local Management of Schools* and a large number of articles on delegated finance. He is joint author with Linda Ellison of *Education Management for the 1990s.*

Linda Ellison MSc is a Senior Lecturer in charge of Education Management at Leeds Polytechnic. She is extensively inolved with programmes of senior management training, particularly for heads and deputies in primary schools. She has also been involved in the provision of staff development on LMS in a variety of LEAs. She is joint author with Brent Davies of *Education Management for the 1990s.*

Managing Primary School Staff
Chris Braund

Following the 1988 Education Reform Act, every primary school has become fully responsible for its own professional and non-professional recruitment and staffing, including appointments, staff management and appraisal, terms and conditions of service, discipline, grievances, dismissal and related matters. The freedom of schools to manage their own affairs means important new legal and practical rights and duties for all school managers. Presented in a user-friendly format, *Managing Primary School Staff* meets the urgent need for practical help on a subject of vital importance for the future success of every school.

Contents: Introduction, effective school leadership, the art of deputising, coordinating the curriculum, appointing, promoting and dismissing teachers and other staff, staff support and development, effective staff coummunication, planning for success, case studies, suggested management exercises, glossary, further reading, index.

Paperback, approx 128 pages, illustrated.

The School Library
Elizabeth King MA ALA

Written by a former Chairperson of the School Library Association, this book appraises the role of school libraries in a changing world — a world in which new ideas, new technology and new initiatives (and financial cutbacks) present a special challenge for the professional. 'A stimulating appraisal of the role of the school library in a changing educational world of cutbacks, information technology and educational reform.' *Junior & Middle School Education Journal.*

Paperback, 112 pages, illustrated.

The School Meals Service
Nan Berger OBE FHCIMA

The importance of the school meals service is becoming better recognised today, following greater interest in diet and health, and the advent of privatisation and what it means for standards of service in the educational system. This new book meets the longstanding need for an introduction to—and defence of—the School Meals Service. Expert, readable and forthright, it reviews key health and management issues for everyone having a professional interest in children's welfare, from head teachers and governors to catering managers and educational administrators.

Contents: Foreword, acknowledgements, the beginnings, what the service is and does, the structure of the service, training, nutrition, organising the production of school meals, the stigma of the free school meal, the competition, the problem of midday supervision, the economics of the School Meals Service, the effects of the Education (No. 2) Act 1980, the role of the Government, the future of the School Meals Service, appendices (organisations, statistics, notes on Scotland and Northern Ireland), chronology, bibliography, index.

'Informative, thought-provoking and controversial.' *Lunch Times*. 'Maori-style cooking has not, to my knowledge, been much practised by our own School Meals Service, though no doubt ungrateful children would have their parents believe otherwise. The kind of folklore perception of school dinners is tackled in Nan Berger's School Meals Service. There is much more to the book than this, however, for it is a thorough and well documented history of the meals service, starting with its origins in the last century and moving on to recent traumas of privatisation and closure.' *Times Educational Supplement*. Nan Berger OBE FHCIMA is former Editor of the *National Association of School Meals Organisers Handbook* and *Hospitality* magazine.

Paperback, 144 pages, illustrated.